MY LIFE
ZERO TO
SIXTY

MY LIFE
ZERO TO
SIXTY

by TERRY BISH

as told to TIM BENNETT

SEL PUBLICATIONS
Syracuse, New York

My Life: Zero to Sixty
Copyright © 2009 by Terry Bish
as told to Tim Bennett

ISBN 978-0-615-33982-5

Published by:
Sel Publications
Syracuse, NY

THIS BOOK IS DEDICATED TO:

. . . all those who think life has passed them by. We all have a story to tell. When we take time to reflect on our lives, we see all the lessons we have learned and remember all the people who have had an influence on us—both good and bad. We also realize that we, too, have an impact on others in one way or another. None of us are perfect. We all make mistakes. However, we hopefully learn from those errors and move on. By doing so, I believe, we can better ourselves and have a positive influence on those around us.

I also dedicate this book to my wife, Charlene, and to my children, Jonathon and Kimberly, whom I love dearly and who put up with all my ways. I thank the Lord for their love and support.

Finally, I want to honor Rudy and June Bish for raising me and being such hard-working parents.

ACKNOWLEDGEMENTS

I would like to thank Tim Bennett for his encouragement to write this book, the hours he spent working with the manuscript, and his ability to put it all together; David Danglis for his help with the cover and layout; Timothy Bleecker PhD for his editorial suggestions; my family for just being who they are; and my Lord and Savior Jesus Christ who has taken me this far on my journey and will one day bring me across the finish line.

CONTENTS:

INTRODUCTION

In the automotive world, performance is measured in many standard ways. Zero to sixty mph from a dead stop is one of the most-used performance tests to measure the quality and the speed of a car or a motorcycle. How fast the test product can go and how well it handles are the focus of this test. A reverse test is also used from 60 to 0 to evaluate how well the test subject can stop.

This book is a snapshot of my life from zero to sixty. In many ways there have been many tests along the road. Some I have passed with flying colors and others have taken me years to pass, while others are yet to come. I am grateful to God that when I have failed a test He has given me two, three, and sometimes even more opportunities to get it right. I am amazed at how fast my life has flown by from childhood to young adult, to middle age to senior citizen—like the gear shifts on a motorcycle or a high-performance car, each one has needed to mesh smoothly with the next.

You will notice from a young age that I have always had a fascination with speed, whether it is with a bicycle, a motorcycle, a car, or a boat. I can't explain why but there is just something about the exhilaration of going fast that I find thrilling. You will notice, too, that there were times in my life when I needed to slow down and stop in order to get a better bearing of where I was going and how to get there.

I continue to be amazed at God's goodness to me and my family. He is a generous God and I have been privileged to own a successful business in transmission repair for over 20 years. I've also enjoyed having a radio program for almost as long. My greatest joy and achievement, however, has been my marriage, which is going on 38 years this September. Charlene, you truly are a gift from God.

Although I would not choose to relive some of the more painful episodes of my life, I am glad that in God's economy nothing is wasted and, in fact, even the most difficult things can always be used to help someone else.

I pray that my successes as well as my failures may be an encouragement to you and give you a glimpse of God's love and grace to a man who doesn't deserve it, but who receives it gladly with open arms.

CHAPTER 1
STARTING THE RACE

I joined the human race in the usual way. I don't remember much about the event, but I guess that's normal. I was born in Johnson City, New York, in May of 1952. You mathematicians in the crowd will quickly deduce that I am 57 years old, not 60, so why the title **Zero to Sixty**? Well, I figure that's close enough and the title fits my life. Plus, I am counting on the fact that this book will still be in print in three years.

Probably the most memorable event of my childhood was the Christmas of 1960 when I was eight years old. My family of six (I am the oldest child with two younger brothers and a sister) had made the short trip from our farmhouse in Owego to Central Square, New York to celebrate the holiday with my mother's parents. Two things made the event extra special. One was the abundance of snow that had fallen that year and two was the extreme generosity of my grandparents who went overboard showering us with gifts and toys. Never before had we received so many presents, and we were happy as bandits as we waved goodbye to grandma and grandpa with our car full of plunder.

Yet, just a week later, all those gifts, as well as everything else we owned as a family, went up in smoke. The furnace had been filled that day with kerosene but for some reason the heat went off nonetheless. Since my dad was working, my mom went into the furnace room to relight it but the match she used bounced off the furnace and landed on the floor, which immediately burst into flames. Apparently, there had been a leak in the fuel line and the floor was covered with kerosene. She came screaming into our room—all four of us slept in the same room together, which was right next to the furnace room—picked up Rudy who was eight months old, grabbed the hand of Christina who was almost three, and yelled at Jerry and me to get out because the house was on fire. She then pushed Jerry and me in front of her and we all raced out into the snow in our bare feet and pajamas. We kept looking back and we could see the flames coming out of the roof as we sprinted to our neighbor's house that was fifty yards away. By the time we reached their front porch the furnace exploded and the whole house blew up, belching up flames of orange into the crisp, winter sky, leaving us homeless in a matter of seconds.

At the time, I was just numb from the shock of it all. Later, I grieved the loss of all those toys—especially the flashlight with the lenses that you could change so you could see different animals on the wall. Looking back, it must have been devastating to my parents just struggling to get by with four young children.

After the fire, since there was no insurance on the house, we were basically at the mercy of our family, neighbors, and charity to give us the essentials. Let's just say my clothes were either too small, too big, or just plain worn. Right after the fire, we moved in with my Uncle Bill and Aunt Charlotte who lived just up the hill from us. But we didn't stay too long because tensions ran high with so many people in one house. My aunt and uncle also had two children and Grandma Bish was living with them too, so it was a full house.

My dad wasn't home the night of the fire because he was working as a night janitor. He took that job after losing the dairy farm we had in Harpersville, New York. The cows had contracted some disease and they could no longer be used as dairy cows, only for meat. Since Uncle Bill had a cleaning business he immediately offered a job to my dad. So my dad went from being his own boss running a successful dairy farm with employees and a hundred cows to working for his youngest brother buffing floors. I'm sure it wasn't an easy transition for him, but he was the type of guy who would do anything to put food on the table for his family. He had ended up losing the farmhouse and another house he owned because he couldn't pay either of the mortgages. After that, my parents' plan had been to rent the house from Uncle Bill in Owego until they had the means to get their own house. Then the house burned down.

I missed the farm though. We not only had a hundred cows but we also had a number of different animals. We had an Ashley, which is a long-horned cow, and my dad used to pick me up and put me on its back. Another animal was a super intelligent Border collie named Spunky who helped round up the herd of cows. It was funny to see that little dog boss those big cows around and get them where they had to go. If my dad thought Spunky was moving them too fast he would jump into the car and beep the horn and the dog would slow down. We even had a pet deer that apparently thought he was a cow, because he would nurse from the cows and then walk back with them in the evening to the barn. When the authorities found out, though, they didn't think it was very funny and said the deer had to go.

When my dad's brother Uncle Ben found out about all the problems at Uncle Bill's, he suggested we move into their house in Whitney Point. He and his family had just bought and renovated another house just up the street and moved into it, which meant that their previous house was available to us. Shortly after that, my dad got a job in construction.

The thing I remember most about that house was the racetrack for stockcars that I could see from my upstairs bedroom window. Jerry and I could easily spend hours watching for accidents where the cars would flip up over the wall of the racetrack. The thing I didn't like was when the ambulance left with the injured drivers and the siren would be so loud it would wake up my baby brother Rudy and he would wail. As the older brother I would have to go downstairs and rock his crib until he fell back to sleep again.

During that time I remember Grandma Bish coming over on the weekends to help take care of us. Unfortunately, I used to give her a hard time. She was only five feet tall and she used to chase me around with a belt, but I was too fast for her. I could get away with being a wise guy with her, but my parents wouldn't have tolerated two seconds of my rebellion.

Meanwhile, I had to get used to being a new kid in rough-looking clothes at a strange school where a lot of kids thought "Terry" was a girl's name. For all intents and purposes my parents could have named me Sue and I don't think it would have been any worse. I probably got in more fights about my name than anything else. Without fail, almost every recess a small group of boys would come and harass me about my name and the fists would start flying. Since I was bigger and stronger than most of them I would always win.

After six months in Whitney Point my parents bought a used trailer—ironically from a lady whose niece I would marry twelve years later. The money came from a fundraiser that a Methodist church in Flemmingville, New York held for our family. We moved back to the property in Owego across from where the house had burned down. Uncle Bill had built a trailer park there and had an empty lot available. My brother Jerry and I had one room with bunk beds and Christeena and Rudy had the other room, while my parents had the master bedroom down on the other end.

It was around this time I started spending a lot of time in the woods. My grandfather had given me a BB gun when I was nine and I would pass hours and hours practicing my aim on birds and rabbits. Birds were easy prey but rabbits required more of a challenge: I had to hit them in the eye to kill them. Out in the country where we lived, everybody, except my dad maybe, hunted and fished and I took to it naturally, even though no one officially taught me.

It was during this time that, on two occasions. I first acknowledged that God existed. The first time was when I was in the bus on my way to school. I was just looking out the window as we were driving through the countryside and I suddenly noticed that there was an order to nature. We passed several sections of open fields and I could see groups of 50 to 100 deer grazing. At another stretch of land I saw people gathering syrup from the maple trees. I was amazed by the wide variety of trees and the colorful display of red, yellow, and orange leaves. When we went by a stream I thought about the fish, too. There just had to be a Creator of all that.

The second time I was convinced God existed, I can't say I was too happy about it. I was out walking down a hill with my BB gun and a sparrow landed right in front of me. I figured this was an easy shot so I pumped my gun and shot at it. But I missed. I couldn't believe it so I pumped it again and fired again. Again I missed. The little bird was oblivious, of course, of what I was trying to do. He just kept hopping and flying merrily down this hedgerow and I was following him and shooting at him. I was trying to somehow get in front of him so I could get a clean shot. But for the life of me I could not hit this bird, and I was becoming totally frustrated because normally when I pulled the trigger the bird dropped, but this bird had some kind of invisible shield around him. Finally, I gave up and raised my fist at God because I knew He must have been the one protecting this bird. To me, there was no other explanation.

It was shortly after this time that we moved our trailer up near Corning Glass Works because the construction company my father worked for had a project up there. We ended up being there for about a year when I was in fourth grade. My main pastimes at this juncture were playing baseball and shooting snakes with my BB gun with Jerry. For some reason the birds must have heard about my arrival so they didn't show up near where we lived. But the snakes were everywhere—Garter Snakes, Timber Rattlers, Black Snakes, and water snakes—which resembled the poisonous Water Moccasins in appearance. There were so many they would be hanging from the trees near the creek bed. If we didn't see any in the trees we could be sure there were some in the leaves along the banks. Fortunately, Jerry and I rarely got bit. When we did it was usually by Garter Snakes because we knew they weren't dangerous. The Water Snakes, however, with their diamond-shaped heads and nasty dispositions, looked mean so we kept our distance. They could also get as big as four feet so we didn't want to mess with them at close range.

We met a truck driver in the trailer park who used to collect rattles from rattlesnakes and he had a cigar box full of them. He used to go out west all the time in his rig, and whenever he saw a dead snake on the road, or one he had run over, he would stop and pick it up. He ran over one that was eight feet long. My brother and I used to hang out with this guy and he told us a lot of his stories of being on the road.

I also started playing little league baseball in Corning. I had a strong arm so I was elected pitcher. It was my first experience with a team sport and I enjoyed the camaraderie. My second passion was flipping baseball cards and accumulating as many as possible while, of course, enjoying the flat pink bubble gum that came with the cards.

The only major problem I had in Corning was when I broke the nose of a kid who lived up the street after he had punched my sister. He was bleeding so badly that his blood filled a towel my mother had used to stop the bleeding. When his father found out what had happened he told me one day when I walked past his house: "I'll kill you if you ever step on my property!"

After my father's job ended in the area, we moved the trailer to Glenn Mary Drive in Owego across from my grandparents on my mother's side. This was out in the country and I returned to spending a lot of time in the woods and fishing in the creek.

I also started working picking berries with my Grandma Hoover, and I liked earning money that I could spend the way I wanted. I was probably around 11. I made a whopping 10 to 11 cents a quart, which I thought was a lot of money for a kid my age.

I did that for a couple of years.

At 12, the same guy who owned the berry patch hired me to work around his apple orchard pruning the trees. One particular day he had worked me really hard and this led me to my first major bike accident. I was on my way home on my bike, coasting down a hill, when I decided to close my eyes for a few seconds. When I opened them, however, the landscape had changed and now an old lady was on the road in front of me coming back from her mailbox. I couldn't stop quickly enough and I ran into her. Fortunately, I didn't hit her hard enough to knock her down, but was she mad.

This was one of many bicycle mishaps. I had worse. As a kid I loved speed so accidents came with the territory. I recall distinctly one day when I wanted to see how fast I could go on a stretch of road near my house. It was a steep hill a half-mile long with S-turns that led to a single lane bridge over a 30-foot drop to the creek. I took the bike to the top of the hill and let her rip. I was rolling along at a good clip with the wind in my face. I sped through the first part of the S, and then I came out of the second part and what did I see but a woman sitting in a car in the middle of the one-lane bridge. It suddenly dawned on me that the car was not moving and she was not making any effort to move. I noticed as well that there was not enough room to get by her and my only alternative seemed to be a 30-foot plunge into the creek below. So I did the only thing I could do and I hit the brakes. The bike then began fishtailing and I began sliding dangerously as I was getting closer and closer to her car. Unfortunately, when I swerved to the side of the road the gravel caused the bike and me to go down and I fell off and found myself sliding down the pavement on my backside toward the side of the bridge. It was so hot sliding on the pavement I was gritting my teeth to endure the pain. Meanwhile I was thinking: *This is not good. What if I don't stop at the bridge and I go over?*

After what felt like an eternity, I finally came to an abrupt halt by hitting the bridge abutment. Much to my dismay, from my trip down, half of my pants had been completely ripped off. When I got up there were brush burns on my leg and my left hindquarter was bare, numb and bleeding. Suddenly I noticed the car had moved, and now the window was down and the woman was asking me, "Do you need help? Are you okay?" I felt like saying, "Not really. I almost died by going over the cliff because you didn't move your car." Instead, I just shook my head and muttered, "No. I'm okay," picked up my battered wheels and pushed the bike home.

Another time I did go off a bridge on my bike near my house. I had turned around to yell at one of my siblings about something as I was approaching a little bridge, and when I faced front again I noticed too late that my bike had veered seriously to the right. Immediately I disappeared from sight and dropped 10 feet into the shrubs and brush alongside a stream. Everybody, including my brother and sister, came running to the edge to see if I had survived. I felt stupid but I wasn't hurt bad. I was just lucky I hadn't poked my eyes out with one of those branches.

My most interesting stunt probably was when I was trying to be funny; I pulled a wheelie in front of my Aunt Pat's car to impress her, and the wheel fell off because it was too loose. As you can imagine, when the front end came down there was nothing there, and the forks went right into the pavement. This was one of my first involuntary flying escapades and I can't say I liked the experience. I sailed over the handlebars and somersaulted right in front of my aunt's car in the other lane, where she had been jamming on the brakes to avoid hitting me. She just shook her head, rolled down the window, and gave me a few choice words.

But I was doing more profitable things besides nearly killing myself on my bike by the time I was 13. Some local trappers had told Jerry and me how to trap muskrats on the creek in front of our property, and it turned out to be a gold mine. We ran a half-mile trap line before and after school every day, and we could sell the furs for $1.25 or $1.50 apiece to the local sporting goods store. No matter how many we brought to Everett, the owner, he would buy them all. He couldn't lose. He would sell the furs for a profit and the money he gave us we would spend in his store.

We did have a close call, though, one winter running the trap line. It was twenty below zero that morning, and Jerry slipped into the icy creek while he was checking one of the traps. Although it wasn't that deep he was totally drenched, and I knew that we were far enough away from home that he would not make it back without becoming hypothermic. I immediately took my dry clothes off and put on his wet clothes. I knew even at that age that if your body temperature dropped below a certain degree you would go into shock and die. I am sure it was my experience in Boy Scouts that prepared me for that day. Our leaders ingrained in us that someone could freeze to death in less than twelve minutes. As a result we both made it safely back to the house.

Since I was the oldest it was always my responsibility to watch over the others, which sometimes posed a great challenge for me. It seemed my youngest brother, Rudy, and sister, Teena, would go out of their way to aggravate me. For example, if I said, "Don't do that!" they would be sure to do it. And if told them not to touch something they would make it a point to touch it. And sometimes I would just lose it and react angrily. One time we were outside and Rudy was giving me a hard time as usual, and so I picked up a rock and threw it at him. The rock caught him just underneath his nose and tore that piece between the nostrils right off. It also curved up and gave him a nice gash just under his eye. When my mother got home and saw him with all the bandages, she turned to me with a stern look and said, "How did this happen?"

"Oh, I was just throwing rocks up in the air and one came down on his face." She didn't look necessarily convinced but she did not pursue the subject any further.

Of course, I had strictly said to my brother earlier, "You say something: You die." After a quick trip to Dr. Nichols' office and a few stitches later, he was good as new.

It seemed like every time we turned around we were taking

Rudy to the hospital for something. One time sledding, Jerry and I hit him with a sled because he just got in the way. He had gone before us and was on the ground in our path, and we clipped him in the ear. It was so bad his ear was hanging on by only a sliver of skin. I think that time he probably got a hundred stitches. Another time we were sleigh riding and he didn't see that there was a pitchfork buried in the snow, and it went right through the calf of his leg. When we got home and he lifted his pant leg, I could see his boot was filled to the top with blood—I had nothing to do with it and I mean that. He just managed to do that on his own.

But back to my first business of selling furs. It was great. My brother and I would catch the muskrats in the traps, skin them, tan them, and then take them down to the sporting goods store where Everett always bought everything we had. We also liked to hang out there and listen to the older guys tell their hunting and fishing stories. We always enjoyed the atmosphere with all the hunting and fishing paraphernalia and the smell of leather and gun oil. Everett would be behind the counter next to the cash register, and we would all be standing around listening to whoever was speaking.

Usually, half way through the stories, Everett would stop the proceedings and suggest we all flip a coin to see who would buy the sodas for everyone. If you were the odd man out you bought. Some of these tales seemed kind of tall, but these guys were excellent storytellers so we didn't mind. These were the kind of guys who would work for the county on the road crew but would quit their jobs in the fall and just hunt, trap and fish for four months. They just figured they could make more money doing that than with the county. As kids we would have given an arm and a leg to do that rather than going to school. In my opinion, these guys knew how to live.

When it came to fishing or hunting, however, they didn't respect any limits or laws. For example, when the salmon and trout were running they taught us how to pull trout from underneath the creek banks with our bare hands as the fish were spawning. For them, it wasn't for sport but for food for their families. It was the same thing with hunting of any kind. They took what they needed and ignored the law.

All these men by today's standards would be considered poor, but their lives were rich in their relationships and outdoor adventures. They had humble homes, but it was not uncommon to have expensive guns or dogs. Most of these dogs were not only pets but were used for hunting and making money in contests—primarily coon hunting tournaments. All these experiences served as great fodder for their colorful stories. I was amazed at how they could make simple and everyday events hilarious and interesting. For example, one guy told us about a time when he was hunting late in the afternoon and shot a deer around dusk. It was too dark to gut the deer and he didn't want to get caught after the legal closing time, so he quickly dragged the deer to his car and threw it in the trunk. When he got home he opened the trunk, only to have the deer leap out and run away. Apparently he had only grazed the deer in the head and knocked it out instead of killing it. The incident startled him so badly that he tripped and fell over backwards. To hear him tell the story and act it out had all of us howling with laughter.

When we got back to Owego, I continued playing baseball and decided to join the Boy Scouts. I was grateful for the latter organization, because it allowed me to meet a lot of kids my age and helped me to learn a great deal about nature and surviving in the woods. We would do campouts once a month on the weekend and then for a whole week in the summer. I don't know how my mother did it, but she always had the money for me to go to camp. In fact, thanks to her, I never missed a campout the whole time I was in Boy Scouts. I guess you could say that was my way to get out of the house—away from everybody and everything. Each year I kept getting awards for never missing a campout, and after five years I got a special certificate for not being absent one time.

I must say, too, that I had some exposure to religion when I was in Boy Scouts, but, to be truthful, it was a little confusing to me. For example, whenever we camped out somewhere we would always go to church. When there were Protestant and Catholic churches available, the Catholics would go to their church and the Protestants would go to theirs. Sometimes, however, we would go to a Catholic church when there wasn't a Protestant one nearby. It would always baffle me to see these kids showing so much respect for the Catholic rituals and then later seeing the same ones sneaking wine into our camp. I guess it was my first experience with hypocrisy and I can't say it impressed me.

But I never really was the type of guy to run with the pack. I remember there was a guy named Steve who all the scouts used to pick on except me. I knew what it was like to get picked on, and I didn't want to do it to someone else. One night they were chasing him all over the woods and they wouldn't let up. Anyway, Steve came bursting into my campsite, obviously nervous and frantic, and I asked him, "What's going on?"

"Everybody is after me," he said.

"Quick. Go into my tent and lay low," I said.

So he went into my tent. Meanwhile, my tent mate and I were outside keeping the campfire going, and all of a sudden about a dozen kids came running into the clearing yelling, "Where's Steve? Where's Steve?"

"Don't know. Didn't see him," I said.

They took off into the woods whooping and hollering, trying to find him. They were playing a kind of bullies' hide and seek. They let the kid have about five minutes to get away, and then they chased him all over creation. It was about an hour and half later that Lou, our scoutmaster, came looking for Steve, and I told him that he was hiding in my tent. Lou told me later that he thought it was a good deed that I had done by hiding the guy.

I worked hard on earning merit badges and I made it to the rank of Life. I was also nominated by the leaders to join the Order of the Arrow, which was a special group within the Boy Scouts. On the initiation weekend I was dropped off at night in the woods with a knife and two matches. My goal was to build a shelter and have a fire going before the leaders returned two or three hours later. Unfortunately, it had rained the entire day of my initiation and dry wood was hard to find. But I knew the secret. All I had to do was find some wood and keep shaving it until I got to the dry part. I knew that water takes a long time to completely penetrate a piece of wood, and I didn't have any problem making kindling. For the shelter I found two trees that had been blown over and built a roof by placing branches from other trees over them. Challenges like those I excelled at and I liked the discipline.

The adults leading the troop really took an interest in training the scouts. They gave us a lot of information on how to survive in the woods, do outdoor cooking, use a compass, read a map, and tie knots. The scoutmaster and all the other men took things seriously, and we really had a good time learning about everything from First Aid to Marksmanship.

I am indebted to the Boy Scouts for teaching me leadership skills and the fundamentals of life. Everything is based on helping others. How can you go wrong with that? One of the mottos I learned there still serves me today: *Be Prepared.* Even now I tend to be over prepared rather than under prepared, which has helped me tremendously in the business world.

When I was 14, I worked at a Boy Scouts summer camp in Ithaca called Camp Barton, from the end of June to the end of August. It was the first time I spent so much time away from home. When I look back it was kind of odd: I never called home and nobody ever came to see me. Still, I loved being in the woods all that time, and I honed my skills in archery and learned sailing.

Unfortunately, my dad and I never did much together. He was working all the time, and I cannot even remember ever going on a family vacation with him. One thing he did find time for, though, was watching me play baseball. I was a pretty good baseball player and I used to pitch and play outfield. I also wasn't a bad hitter. In fact, I almost played on the all-star team, but when it came down to another kid and me, the other kid got it. My parents were convinced the selection was biased because they thought I was the better player. They voiced their opinion and I appreciated their support, but it didn't change anything. We lost that fight, but little did I know bigger fights were looming on the horizon.

CHAPTER 2
DEALING WITH THE ROAD HOGS

In any race there are those who like to own the track. So it is in life and also in school. Growing up as a kid from a family that moved a lot, fighting just came with the territory. In elementary school it was my name that caused problems. In junior high it was the fact that I was new in school and that I lived outside of town. I guess you could say I was seen as the country boy in the town school of Owego. I was big for my age at 15 and weighed 155, so I was not a little kid. Plus, I did a lot of physical exercise by helping neighboring farmers, so I was broad shouldered. Yet, although I was confident that I could take care of myself, I still didn't relish the daily insults and threats I got.

Sometimes the taunts would start early, as soon as I got to school. On sunny days we would be obligated to stand outside of the school after we got off the bus until the bell rang for homeroom class. When it was cold or it rained we were herded into the gym and waited there. By the way things were going I knew I could stay neutral for only so long. There was a group of bullies who felt compelled to test my physical prowess and to see what I could do. I was somewhat intimidated by these guys, because their reputation had preceded them and I knew some of them could throw a punch. In fact, I knew Rick, the lead bully, had a father who boxed and had also taught him a few things. I never enjoyed fighting and I would try to walk away from a fight if I could, but in some situations I couldn't.

One such incident occurred on a rainy day when the students were filing into the gym. We had to walk down the stairs to get to the gym and there was this group of ten tough guys waiting for me on two sides at the landing. When I walked through they all punched me. Their fists, for the most part, just glanced off my body, so I just ducked my head and went forward.

When we got into the gym I went to the opposite side with two of my friends who were following me. They asked me if I was okay and I said, "Yeah, no problem," but the other group kept staring at us and whispering among themselves. Finally, one of them, a kid named Guy, came over and said, "Hey, Bish. My buddy over there wants to fight you. Whattaya say?" I looked over to see who the guy was, and when I saw it was John I said, "Sure." John was tall, probably six inches at least taller than I was, but I could see in his face that he didn't seem too thrilled about the encounter and I figured I had a good chance to beat him.

When we faced each other in the ring that had formed around us, he just came out swinging wildly and missed every time. In fact, every time he swung I would lean back and then step forward and punch him directly in the face. We repeated this sequence five or six times and each time I connected solidly. After about the sixth punch, his eyes started to close and he became visually impaired.

Finally, a number of teachers came blasting through the crowd, but not one teacher laid a hand on me. I was a participant in this fight and nobody did or said a thing to me. Instead, two teachers grabbed John and slammed him up against the wall and then hauled him away. Apparently, he had been a real wise guy and was not appreciated very much by the faculty.

I was surprised only one teacher said something to me, and that was the gym teacher. He just said, "Good fight, Bish." So I just went to my homeroom class. I wasn't there for five minutes before I heard over the loud speaker: "Terry Bish. Report to the main office." When I arrived at the principal's office, John was already sitting in a chair with a badly swollen face and the principal started scolding me: "Look what you've done to this boy. He could be seriously injured."

At first I didn't say anything, but then offered something like, "I didn't start it." I didn't want to mess with the principal because he was a no nonsense kind of guy. It was obvious he didn't like what I had done to John's anatomy and he was probably wondering what he was going to say to John's parents. After a few minutes he let me go. I got detention for one day while John was suspended for three.

I thought it was kind of strange that I didn't get into more trouble. Usually if you have two students fighting, both of them would be grabbed and sent to the principal's office. The only thing I could figure at the time was that maybe this kid was just getting the punishment he deserved.

I learned later that Rick was going to trip me as I was backing up to block some of John's swings, but one of my friends intervened and said, "Just let them fight."

Rick, the ringleader, eventually got into a fight with a much smaller, muscular guy and that short guy beat the snot out of him. I heard that nothing he threw at his opponent had any effect, and every time the powerhouse landed a punch he split the bully's face. Apparently, after such a humiliation the air came out of his sails and he didn't consider himself as tough as he had thought. I guess the truism learned here is: *There is always someone tougher than you are.*

After my big fight, most of the bullies left me alone except Guy, the boy who had challenged me to fight his friend. He kept coming up to me and saying, "I'm gonna take you out back and I'm gonna clean your clock, Bish." Finally, I had enough of his threats and the next time he taunted me I said, "Okay, Guy. Let me know when you're ready and we'll go out back." That was the last time he said anything to me.

A few years later, however, Guy became a Christian and his attitude toward me greatly changed: He even started saying hello to me. Before his conversion, the only thing I got from him was insults. Now, his whole demeanor had softened and he was even friendly. At the time I was just bewildered by his night and day behavior.

CHAPTER 3
GETTING UP TO SPEED

When I was around 15, my mom opened her own restaurant called the *Shady Lawn*. She always excelled at cooking and the idea had been bouncing around in her head for quite some time. She had learned how to cook for large groups from working at several college kitchens and at the Ramada Inn. When she saw the "For Rent" sign in the window as she was taking me to a lawn-mowing job, she turned to me and asked, "Terry, if I rented this restaurant, would you help me run it?"

"Sure, Mom," was all I said. The next thing I knew I was learning how to cook, clean, and scoop ice cream. Out of necessity, all of my other side jobs like bailing hay, working in the orchard, and mowing lawns fell by the wayside. The restaurant was located at a convenient spot on the corner of Route 38 and Route 96, just before the bridge in Owego, so after we opened people came to get mom's good home cooking.

In fact, some people liked her food so much they would come from thirty miles away to buy a submarine sandwich. She had this super recipe for rotisserie chicken, and all the ingredients had to be minutely measured. She also added ice cream to the menu, and my dad and I would get into arguments because he thought my scoops were too generous. One time he got so mad he walked to the cash register, grabbed a handful of coins and threw them on the floor, and said, "That's how much money you just gave away!" Personally, I thought the big portions drew the people and then they would buy other things, so I didn't let his tirade change my habits.

I worked there until I was 17. I didn't get paid, but if I needed or wanted something I knew my mom would get it for me. When I got my driver's license my parents said, "We haven't paid you since you started working at the restaurant, so we want to get you your first car."

It was funny my mom had been hiding away an enormous number of half dollars, and when she gave it to me the sum came to $500. Apparently I had said in my father's hearing that I really wanted a Corvette. After that dad kept his eyes open for a good deal for me and declared one day that he saw three Corvettes for $150 a piece that I might want to take a look at. Although I was excited about possibly getting my dream so cheaply, I held my enthusiasm in check—something had to be wrong. And there was: The cars were *Corvairs,* not Corvettes. When I said, "Sorry, Dad, I think I'll pass," he got a little hot under the collar. He meant well. He just didn't know the difference between a Corvair and a Corvette. Obviously, my dad wasn't a real car guy. He just worked a lot.

I was determined to get a sports car, and even though I didn't find a Corvette in my price range I did find a black TR3 Triumph. The motor sounded cool and it was fast. It ran well and I had a ball learning how to stick shift, leave rubber in second and third gear, and negotiate turns at high speeds. In my neck of the woods, we got around in whatever we could. Nobody had a lot of money. To give you an idea of how desperate we were at times, we knew a guy with a tractor (an N9 Ford, which is about half the size of a regular tractor), and we would convince him to take us where we wanted to go because you didn't need a license to drive farm equipment on the roads.

Another major event that happened when I was 17 was winning the "Biggest Buck Contest" put on by the sporting goods store where we sold the muskrat furs. The deer I bagged was a 6-point buck that weighed 140 pounds dressed out. I got him with a bow and arrow and I couldn't have been prouder. I won the $100 and now I had a story of my own to tell.

My parents didn't know, but I would never go to school on opening day of hunting season, and it didn't matter which animal it was —rabbit, squirrel, pheasant, or deer. Teachers would even say to me, "Oh Bish is here. Must not be an opening day for anything today." I would just forge an excuse letter that I was sick. It was just a coincidence that I was sick every Monday when a new season opened.

Truth be known, I wasn't a good student and I even failed fifth grade—probably because we moved around so much. But the fact was, I just didn't like school so I didn't apply myself. Of course, my parents would discipline me with a belt for my bad report cards, but I was incorrigible. I just preferred hunting and fishing to sitting cooped up in a classroom. When I got my own car I skipped classes all the time. That's when I would take off some afternoons and be driving fast somewhere experimenting with my fishtailing techniques around curves. I only had to outrun the local police four or five times and the State Police twice. I am not saying that, of course, to encourage speeding or avoiding the police, that's just who I was at the time.

It was around this time, too, that I bought my first snowmobile, which was red and made by Scorpion. I thought it was the coolest machine ever invented. Ever since they had come out, a few years earlier, I wanted one. Back then they were the goofiest looking things and they weren't very stable either. Regardless, once I had one I just had to do a stunt near my house. On Glen Mary Drive there is a wide sweeping turn just before the bridge and the snowplows had created a large four-foot pile of snow against the guardrail. There was a ten-foot drop on the other side and I wanted to gun the snowmobile over the guardrail and fly as far as I could on the other side. So I accelerated to the maximum, which was probably around 45 mph, and hit the snow bank.

I wanted to capture the great feat with a photograph, so I posted my brother Jerry with a camera where he could get a good shot.

As I went over the rail I must have been 15 feet in the air. Everything was going according to plan until I hit the ground. The snowmobile started rocking back and forth and I fell off, but I was going so fast when I hit the ground that I somersaulted multiple times right next to the sled. I hadn't even given it a thought that I could have just gone right into the guardrail and been seriously injured. That's what happens normally when you hit a guardrail going 45 mph, but I was just sure that I would go up and over when I hit the bank.

Later, in the fall of my seventeenth year, I got a job at a local hotel restaurant where I was the third person hired. My first task was to get the rooms ready for the future occupants. So I hung pictures, assembled beds, and put tables together, or whatever else needed doing. When the hotel officially opened up, I worked as a busboy and made good money between the hourly rate and the tips.

Eventually, I was able to save enough to upgrade my car to a TR4. I used to practice how fast I could go in that car, and I actually spun it around a few times going around a curve too fast. I used to practice on this one particular curve, and every time I would go around it I would go a little faster until one day the back end broke loose and I was sliding toward a telephone pole going backwards at 55 mph. To reduce the direction I just jammed the stick shift down into first and then just tacked the engine out and popped the clutch and let it go. The wheels started to spin and I was sliding backwards and the wheels were spinning forwards, and I got within six inches of that telephone pole before the car started going forward again and I went as fast in the other direction as I had been going the other way. The funny thing is I never panicked. My heart never started beating fast or anything.

Later, I learned how to further hone my speed driving skills when a teacher, who had a 125 Fiat Spider, invited me to go up to the Greene Airport go-cart track. They opened this track up once a month on weekends for sports cars. I used to take my TR4 up there and race Fiats and MG's. It was a single car run so they would just time us. I came in sixth place a couple of times and won some plaques. That was my first experience driving around on a track. Actually, I watched guys roll their cars out there. You could really mess your car up. Of course, some of us had to drive our cars home, but some of these guys brought them in on trailers because they had really nice cars like Porsches that were set up just for racing. I was impressed with them especially because they could actually lift a front wheel four inches off the ground going around the turns.

I almost got nailed one time practicing my speeding around a curve near my house. It wasn't that dangerous, I rationalized, because I could see if anyone was coming across the open land at the curve and there were no houses nearby, which meant the worst that could happen was that I would go into a field. So here I was going around the curve sideways, and just up a couple hundred yards there was a stopped police car.

It must have been quite a shock to the police officer to be talking peaceably with a friend when all of a sudden he sees and hears a car come screeching around the corner. At that point I was pretty much committed so I just hung in there. Then I saw the police officer and the guy staring at me. I wasn't worried, because it was common knowledge that the local police cars were six-cylinder Chevy station wagons with a top speed of 95 mph that anybody could outrun with a decent engine, but I couldn't slow down if I was going to lose him, so I just straightened out and blew right by them. It was probably a 35 mph speed zone and here I was doing 65 or 70 mph.

Of course, when I looked in my rear-view mirror the policeman had his lights on and he was coming after me. I kept going into downtown Owego and there was a car at the red light. Since the Triumph was small I squeezed between this car and the curb, and I drove by it and into town. I quickly parked and got out, because I had heard somewhere that if they didn't catch you in the car there was nothing they could do. So I started walking down the street like I was going for a stroll. The policeman pulled up next to me and said, "If I ever see you do that again I am taking you to jail, and don't you ever try to outrun me again." He basically read me the riot act right there on the spot. I thought about playing dumb and saying, "Oh me? I was just walking down the street." But I decided not to press my luck and I nodded my head and carried on.

Then, not even a week later, I was coming down Fifth Avenue, heading out of town at a high rate of speed, and I passed this same officer at the apex of the turn. Same guy. Different place. I'm thinking, *Oh, crap. I know this guy isn't going to just let me go*, so I made a quick U-turn and came back down just as fast going back to town, and we passed at the exact same place. His lights were going and as I passed him he was looking at me and I was looking at him. By the time he found a place to turn around, though, I was gone. I just went down a couple of side streets and found a parking lot and I jumped out of the car. My goal was to run into Bernie's Bar and hide. It was a bar where a bunch of us used to hang out and I figured the policeman wouldn't find me there. As I was heading towards the bar, however, who do I run into but my mom.

"Oh, hi Terry, what are you doing here?"

I am mortified by this freak encounter and I just want to get out of sight before the cop comes careening around the corner with his siren on and his lights flashing.

"Oh, yeah. Hi, Mom. What's up?"

"I was just doing some errands downtown. What are you doing?"

"Ah . . . Ahh," I stuttered, and then made up some wild story, which I don't think she believed, and she finally went on her way. The whole time we were talking, I couldn't help looking around her shoulder to make sure no new vehicles had showed up on the scene. After she left I waltzed into the bar and he didn't catch me.

One of my fastest cars during high school was a Ford Falcon with a 289 engine. My neighbor helped me soup it up. He had a high-performance Corvette, and we worked my engine over with a high rise intake manifold with a four-barrel, and headers with "Purple Hornies." You could hear me coming from a quarter of a mile away. I could actually pull wheelies with that car. It was hard telling exactly how fast I was going in it, though, because the speedometer didn't work.

Then one day a sheriff came into my mom's diner, and we started talking and I confessed to him that my speedometer didn't work. He said, "You know that's illegal not to have a working speedometer." I told him I had a pretty good idea how fast I was going, but he insisted that I come out to Route 38 and he would use his radar to see how fast I was going. This was a stretch of highway where policemen would often plant themselves because there was a half-mile downhill stretch of road that is straight as an arrow, and many people would go over the speed limit by the time they covered the distance. So he said, "Well, I am going to go up there and sit, so why don't you come by and I'll clock you to see how close you are."

I thought this would be a great opportunity to see how fast my car would go so I followed him up there a few minutes later and I put that pedal to the metal. I had a lot of time to build up speed before I passed him so I knew I was really flying. When I came back to the police car he was mad and that's an understatement. He said, "Do you know, son, how fast you were going?"

"I don't know. My speedometer doesn't work."

"You were going 135 mile per hour!"

I was proud of my car, but I didn't want to show it. I just put on a bewildered face and said, Oh, really?" Fortunately, he didn't give me any more than a tongue-lashing and just let me go.

One thing I enjoyed about working at the hotel restaurant was it really provided me with a good income. When I turned 18 I could also serve alcoholic drinks, so I was promoted to being a waiter, which meant even more money. Remember this was the day when making $100 a week was a lot of money and my teachers were only making $125. I was working four nights a week and making $200 a week. It wasn't long before I upgraded to a new 1969 Camaro. I really wanted a Corvette but I couldn't find one, which was probably a good thing. I did see a Corvette two weeks after I bought the Camaro with a 427 engine and 435 horse, which is now probably worth a million dollars. It was a convertible with all the bells and whistles and power everything. I tried to sell the Camaro so I could buy the Corvette, but I couldn't find any takers on the Camaro. It was a 1969, so it was a nice car with a four speed and a 327 engine.

I knew I had to do something with the Camaro when I drove the car home from the dealer. I got on what was then the new Route 17 going from Binghamton to Owego—a brand new road that was nice and smooth. I drove all the way back to Owego going only 112 mph. That was as fast as that car would go. I found my buddy who had helped me with the Ford Falcon and I told him, "Hey, I got this Camaro that's really slow." He just said, "Well, we can fix that." So he started modifying the engine. We changed out the intake manifold and added a four-barrel and changed the headers with dual exhaust. Eventually, we got it to go over 130 mph too. This guy was amazing with cars. I was really impressed with what he could do. To give you an idea, he had a Corvette that could do wheelies in first, second and third. The whole front end would literally lift up and go into the other lane every time he changed gears. I'd never seen anything like it. He also put a '57 Chevy drag car together that he licensed for ten days, the time you had before inspection. The only reason he put plates on it was so he could go downtown and pull wheelies. He could pull a massive wheelie and keep it up all the way down the street. This car was set up for the strip and not street legal.

When I turned 18 I began to make up for lost time. Some guys say they started drinking at 14, but I never did at that age. I was in Boy Scouts and tried to behave myself and do the right thing. But by the time I reached 18 there were guys I knew who went to Viet Nam so I just wanted to have a good time before it was too late. Even my buddy who helped me with the cars went. When he returned he wasn't the same person. The Corvette went into the barn and I don't know if he ever got it out again.

As time went on I was more rough looking with cut-off jean vests and a motorcycle. I also started hanging out with bikers. During that time the motorcycle gangs were the Magellans and the Hells Angels, and I knew guys in both groups. One guy thought I was getting too close to his wife, so he told me to buzz off or it could be dangerous for my health. He had come home one day and I was at his house, so I listened and backed off. His wife was a friend of mine and I knew both of her brothers, but you didn't mess with these guys or you could be history. These guys were bad dudes. I wasn't doing the really bad stuff they were doing, but they were definitely not a good influence. We would sit around smoking marijuana and drinking.

Donny, a friend who married my cousin, also went to Nam but he didn't come back alive; a sniper killed him. We had gone hunting together many times and he had given me one of his prized "Blue Tip" hunting dogs before he left overseas, so his death shook me up quite a bit. I figured it was only a matter of time before it came to be my turn. This was when I started thinking about the meaning of life. Some students at school would talk to me about Jesus, but their message just didn't register at the time. Probably the only person I really listened to was the sister of a friend of mine named Jody, and that was because I thought she was good looking. Her brother, Skip, however, was far from the Lord. He was a muscular, vertically-challenged guy who suffered from short man's disease. In other words, he had to prove to himself and everybody else that his size meant diddley squat when it came to toughness. To give you an idea of the kind of guy he was, when we went into a bar together he would systematically pick out the biggest guy there, drag him outside and beat him up. Nobody ever stopped him. Everybody was afraid of him. He was one of those guys you couldn't hurt. You could hit him in the head with something and he would look at you like, "Okay. Now what are you going to do?"

Besides hunting, I was also in a rock group. My mom had asked me when I was 12 what I wanted to do in life, and when I responded "to be a musician," she went out and bought me a good Epiphone guitar. I taught myself how to play, and when I was seventeen I joined a rock band. These guys were pretty good musicians, and sometimes I wonder what became of them. I know the keyboard player is now a doctor. Another guy could play just about any instrument you could imagine. It was here that I first started experimenting with drugs. At that time, I don't think we really understood how dangerous this could be, with the exception of heroine. Three guys I knew eventually died from overdoses. I smoked my share of marijuana and also tried LSD and speed. I remember one summer I was just wasted the whole summer. I was making a ton of money so I could afford it. I was also driving a new car and wearing nice clothes. In the eyes of my peers, I guess, I had it made.

Since my parents struggled to make ends meet most of the time, when I started raking in the bucks I liked to spend them. Though mom and dad worked hard, it was still pretty tough keeping their heads above water financially with four kids. Dad was working construction and mom's restaurant was doing okay, but I can't say I was very appreciative of all that they provided for me—like most teens I guess I just wanted what other kids had. One thing I can say that I learned from my parents, though, was to be a hard worker.

I also saw how money seemed to be the biggest issue my parents fought about, and I hated getting dragged into those battles. Sometime during my childhood, either consciously or sub-consciously, I vowed that I would not be poor, and when I started making good money at 18 as a waiter, I moved out. Another waiter at the Inn said one day, "Hey Terry, I have this apartment above a bar with two bedrooms, and if you want to split the rent with me, I'll let you have the other bedroom." It was my ticket out so I took it.

My mother was upset that I moved out, but she didn't make an issue out of it. Maybe she figured it would cut down on expenses with one less mouth to feed. I don't know. I can't say communication was ever a priority with my parents. They could yell pretty well, but no one ever talked. In other words, everybody could hear, but no one could listen.

I stayed in contact with them, of course, but probably most of my interaction with them was at my mom's restaurant. I would stop by for the good food and to let her know I was okay. By that time she even opened up her second diner. In one she served lunch, supper, and ice cream, and closed down at 9 p.m. In the other one she served all three meals.

In the hotel business there's a lot of stuff going on behind the scenes. Back in the seventies at my establishment there were a lot of drugs, parties, and sex going on. It seemed everybody in that business had side jobs and some of them were not always legal. One guy, believe or not, even started running a prostitution ring out of the hotel. He was fired, but that's just to show you what kind of environment it was. The bartender was also selling drugs.

CHAPTER 4
LIVING IN THE FAST LANE: RUNNING ON EMPTY

Materially, I guess you could say I had it made. I was wearing nice clothes, eating in nice restaurants, driving nice cars, and drinking good liquor and wine. But I wasn't content inside and everything was uncertain. My friends were going to Viet Nam; people I knew were dying; and now it seemed even my teachers didn't like me. It could have been because of my cocky attitude at school or jealousy over my good income. Some teachers would pull me aside and ask me point blank, "Are you really making $200 a week?" I'd say, "Yeah, and I only pay taxes on my hourly wage of $1.35 and the rest is cash." I could understand their frustration. It didn't seem fair that they were working so hard for less money than a teenager working only part time.

Meanwhile, I was in this messed up state of mind and Jody kept inviting me to her church. Even though I thought she was great, I still wasn't ready for the church scene. So my responses were non-committal and profound like, "Ahhh . . . I don't know."

Amazingly, her brother Skip eventually straightened out, but he first had to get into a situation where his brawn could not save him. While I just experimented occasionally with drugs, Skip used them constantly. In fact, it got so bad he started having hallucinations even when he wasn't on drugs. At one point they had to send him to a mental institution to figure out what to do with him. He was so unstable he was afraid that he would harm himself. He was a good friend of mine, so I was deeply affected by this turn in his life, but I had absolutely no power to help him.

Another tragedy also shook me up during that time. A group of teenagers had been out for a joy ride in a TR4, like the one I had owned, and ended up flipping it over. One of the girls riding in the back was decapitated. What made it worse was that I had even dated this girl. Later it was discovered that they had been doing drugs beforehand.

Then there was the time when I almost got busted myself. I was sitting in this guy's car from work getting high on weed, and a police car showed up and blocked our car so we couldn't get out. Little did I know that the guy who was driving was a big-time drug dealer. To put it mildly, we panicked, and then quickly locked all the doors. Someone asked, "What are we going to do?" Another responded, "Nothing. We're safe because we have all the doors locked and nobody can get in." Only a stoned person would find comfort in that ridiculous reasoning and we all let out a sigh of relief. Yet, the cop did not get out of his car. He stayed there for what seemed like an eternity and then he just backed up and drove away.

The next day when I went to work, however, the boss came up to me and said, "How come you didn't get arrested?" I said, "Just lucky, I guess." I had no clue what he was talking about and I just punched in for work. Another guy came over to me and said, "You heard about so and so?" I said, "No. What?" And the guy said, "Well, there was a big bust this morning. They busted him and a bunch of other people at five o'clock." So, the guy that I was with the previous evening got canned and I just missed it by a whisker. In all, more than 12 people got picked up that day for drugs. I found out later that when the cop called in with the details of the car they said, "No. Leave him alone. We have the warrants all ready and we want to arrest him tomorrow with some other guys. If you get him now they might take off."

Along with the drug scene there was also the anti-Viet Nam War sentiment that was prevalent in my generation. In reference to the war, however, I can't say I was really an active protester. A lot of guys in my town went in so I just figured if my number came up I would join them. They did have a student protest at my school where a lot of students walked out, but I just used it as an excuse to skip class. I didn't even go to the event.

Although I knew several people who died in Viet Nam and car accidents, some students my age also took their own lives. One death that particularly bothered me was a friend who committed suicide. He seemed like such a nice guy. To look at this guy you would think that he had it made. He came from a decent family and always dressed well and always had a nice car to drive. I, on the other hand, came from a family of lack and I would never even consider killing myself. I just didn't get it. This guy was even popular in school. Instead of being content with all he had, he took a .22 caliber and shot himself in the head. Of all people, why would he do that?

In the fall of 1971, when I was 19, I was tired of school. I had failed a grade, so that's why I was still in high school. I had also spent almost the whole previous summer doing drugs and drinking. I was older than most of the other kids except for a small group of us who had all stayed back a grade or two. Nobody gave us grief because we were bigger and older than everybody. Kids back then were a lot different than kids today. I mean, we were farm boys who used to have contests to see how many feed bags you could carry the length of a barn. We had one guy who could carry five feed bags, which was 400 lbs. How many people do you know who, when they were 17 or 18, could carry 400 lbs. the length of a barn? We were not small guys and even most teachers would not dare mess with us. We weren't punks in the sense that we went around beating people up—except for Skip, of course. He had to prove to everybody he was a tough guy. The rest of us did not. We just knew we could take care of ourselves.

Hunting season was coming around and I got this idea about bear hunting in the Adirondacks. My buddy, Bob, was my bus boy at the restaurant and he had the same hours and days off as I did, so

I made arrangements to stay at my Uncle Mike and Aunt Isabelle's house up in Boonville, New York. It was a spur of the moment thing. We threw the guns in the car along with some clothes and took off. Uncle Mike was one of my dad's brothers, and I remembered that he and my aunt were always glad to have company, so I had no problem calling them up. They quickly said, "Sure. C'mon up." When we got up there, however, we didn't have a clue where to find a bear, and we ended up just driving down a number of country roads.

Around three o'clock in the afternoon we started getting weary of looking at trees and no bear sightings, so we decided to go back to a bar we had passed along the way. We stayed there until closing and somehow made it back to my aunt and uncle's in one piece. They were already asleep, so we just tiptoed through the house to our room and crashed.

The next day we slept in until late morning, and when we finally got up my aunt had a big breakfast of eggs, pancakes, and bacon waiting for us. She did not mention the previous night. She had no rebukes for the late hour we strolled in. She just smiled and served us a hearty meal. After thanking her for the sumptuous breakfast we went back out in search of the elusive bears, but again we didn't encounter any bear brave enough to show himself, so we took the path of least resistance and found another bar. You have to understand that these bars have some pretty rough-looking characters, and they are more of the redneck type than the long hair variety. And here we were two teenagers with long hair leisurely walking into a redneck bar. Back then, bars were pretty much segregated into three categories: biker bars, hippie bars, and farmer bars. And you had better watch out if you tried to cross territorial lines. Well, as soon as we walked into this bar we started getting all this flack, but we were not backing down . . . .

Which reminds me of a bet I had with a buddy one time in Owego. He said, "I don't think you have the guts to go into that farmer bar across the street."

"You're on," I said. One thing I liked was a challenge, so I just walked across the street and made my entrance like it was a free country. Of course, it probably didn't help that I had hair down to my shoulders and a cut-off jeans vest with an upside down flag on the back, but I wasn't known for my social graces. As soon as I entered everybody stopped talking. My goal was to order a beer at the bar, so I headed in that direction, but by the look of things I started to wonder if I would make it.

Meanwhile, all my cronies were craning their necks to see what was going to happen from across the street. Every time a hippie had gone in there in the past he would get physically tossed out into the street, so they were sure I would come flying out any second. I figured I could handle myself for a little while if they jumped me, but some of these farm guys were big. I could feel dozens of eyes boring into me when all of a sudden I heard a voice say, "Hey Terry! Is that you?" I looked toward the voice and it was Don, a guy I knew from school who had just got back from Viet Nam and was wearing his uniform. He said, "Hey, let me buy you a drink!" As soon as they knew I was Don's friend, the rest of them backed off and resumed talking.

But . . . back to the story up in the Adirondacks. It was a similar situation, and Bob and I were getting some serious insults from the regulars, and the tension was building for a fistfight. Then, for some oddball reason I mentioned my Uncle Mike. Someone asked, "Who's your Uncle Mike?"

"Mike Bish," I said.

"Mike Bish. Well, I'll be. Let me buy you a drink."

Immediately, as in the other story, the climate changed and we were "innocent by association." Again, we closed the place down and stumbled back into my aunt and uncle's house in the middle of the night.

The next morning, however, it was as if nothing had happened. My Aunt Isabelle gave us another big, country meal with the same warm smile. After two days, however, we were convinced that the bears were hibernating early that year and we might as well head back to Owego. As we are going out the door she gave me a big hug, then said very sweetly, "Terry, I just want you to have this," and slipped a little booklet into my pocket.

CHAPTER 5
WHAT IS THE RACE ALL ABOUT?

To let you know how hung over I was from the night before, I even let Bob drive my Camaro back to Owego. I found myself just looking out the window thinking to myself: *What am I doing with my life? Where am I going? What is my purpose?* All I could see in front of me was Viet Nam and that my life was going nowhere. Then, for some reason, I put my hand in my pocket and pulled out the little booklet my aunt had given me. The title quickly got my attention: *What Life Is All About.* When I turned the pages it was in a cartoon-type format and followed the life of a guy from birth to death. He finished school. He got married. He found a career. He had children. Yet, throughout his life whenever someone would try to tell him about Jesus Christ and how he could receive eternal life, the guy made up excuses for why it was not the right time. At the end, the man was banished from the presence of God.

The booklet also explained about the good things that would happen if he did choose to live for Christ both here and now, and for all eternity. It talked about how God wanted to have an intimate relationship with everyone and actually wanted to come and live inside us if we would just let him. It had a quote from the Bible that said, "Here I am! I stand at the door and knock. If anyone hears my voice and opens the door, I will come in and eat with him, and he with me" (Revelation 3:20 NIV). As I was reading I couldn't believe it. This was the answer I was looking for—God.

It stirred something deep within me and when we got back Sunday afternoon to Owego I immediately called Jody, who had been inviting me to church, and asked, "What time is the service?"

"We have an evening meeting at 7 p.m. Why don't you come?"

This time I didn't hesitate. "Sure. I'll be there."

So I went to the service and discovered it was a Christian Missionary Alliance church, although the label meant nothing to me. When I got there I couldn't believe it: The church was packed out. I also couldn't get over the atmosphere. I felt something in my spirit. There was a presence of peace and joy. Of course, I had no idea that it was God's presence at the time, but I could feel something was different. People were standing everywhere down the sides and in the back. Then, after some upbeat worship songs, Pastor Mather got up and started to preach. I don't remember his message, but when he asked those who wanted to accept Jesus to come forward I couldn't get to the altar fast enough. I think I ran down there. I knew I had not been living right—the drinking, the drugs, the selfishness, and the womanizing. I didn't have a lot of moral teaching growing up, but I knew without a doubt that these things did not please God.

The leaders of the church then took the people who came to the altar aside and went over the plan of salvation again and answered any questions we might have. When I was done talking with this guy, I turned around and noticed that all the people were back in their places, and the pastor then stuck a microphone in my face and asked, "How do you feel?"

I had to think about it a minute, and then I said the first thing that came into my mind: "I feel clean. I feel new!"

From that day on my life changed and everything felt different. The grass was greener; the sky was bluer. I started reading my Bible in the Gospel of John and I started going to church. It was a whole new world where people were talking in different languages, giving prophesies, and praying for the sick who were actually getting healed.

I eventually called my Aunt Isabelle and told her what had happened and even went up to her church a few times, which was an Assembly of God church. Despite the different denomination, however, the service felt the same to me. The people worshiped the Lord with enthusiasm and the preacher spoke from the Bible.

In the beginning of my faith walk, though, both of my parents thought that I had gotten involved with a cult. My mother even went down to that Christian Missionary Alliance Church where I got saved and voiced her displeasure with the pastor. This has always seemed odd to me: People often are not offended when you are living a wild life but the minute you say you are a Born-Again Christian they think you've gone off the deep end.

Then I started sharing my faith with others. God also began speaking to me when I read the Bible. I would read some verses and it was as though God was saying them right to me for my particular situation. More and more of my friends "got saved" and we would spend a lot of time in church as well as studying the Bible and other Christian books.

I remember trying to tell a friend at school what had happened to me, and the guy couldn't grasp that I was a Jesus freak now. Then I said, "Let's put it this way. It's like if you've never seen the color green before. I could try to explain to you what it looked like but, until you saw it, it would be hard for you to understand. It's the same way with God—until you experience Him for yourself like I did you just won't understand." It must have been the Holy Spirit who gave me this illustration, because all of a sudden he said it now made sense to him. I had experienced the presence of God in my life and he hadn't yet. This kid had known me since the sixth grade and now it was my senior year and he was sure: "This isn't the Terry I know."

It was a time, too, when I could really sense the Lord speaking to me. I remember one time I was sitting at my mom's restaurant because she had to run some errands and needed someone to watch the restaurant for her. Nobody was in the place and I was there sitting by myself reading the Bible when I heard an audible voice: "Call Bob." This was weird. I put my Bible down and looked around the restaurant. Maybe someone had come in and I hadn't noticed. I looked around the room and there wasn't anyone there, so I went back to reading. I heard it again. About the third time I heard "Call Bob" I thought I should just go ahead and do it. I knew that Bob was working that night, but I called him anyway. When I got him on the phone, I said, "So Bob, you've got to work tonight, don't you?"

"Well, funny you should ask because they just gave me the night off. There isn't enough work for me to come in."

"Really. Why don't you come to church with me tonight."

"Okay."

It was that simple. He came to church that night and gave his life to the Lord.

In fact, my relationships with my teachers changed that year too, and they actually liked me. I had a couple of teachers come up to me and say, "Bish, you have really changed." I guess it was pretty dramatic because I started getting good grades, doing my homework, and even showing up for school. I also stopped being sarcastic and being a wise guy—something that teachers everywhere generally appreciate.

I also began visiting this halfway house that Skip opened up with his wife for drug addicts. Skip would give his testimony of being delivered from hallucinations and I would play the guitar. My music also changed as my rock group disbanded and I started learning to play Christian songs.

Sex, though, was a little more difficult to sever. Girls from my past started coming out of the woodwork and all of them seemed to want to "get serious." I tried to avoid them like the plague, but the opportunities for sex seemed to increase tenfold after my experience and I can't say I always resisted. Unfortunately, although I was able to give up the drugs and alcohol pretty easily, sex was a lot harder.

I knew I had to change when Bob and his girl friend, Wendy,

just stopped by unannounced at my place after church to see why I wasn't at the service. The reason I didn't go was because I was in bed with a girl. I was embarrassed, and after a time I came to the conclusion that the one-night stands had to go, too.

It was at this time that Bob thought I should get a steady girl friend, so he and Wendy took great delight in arranging blind dates for me. The first girl didn't work out, but the second one was with Charlene. When I first met her I thought: *Now here is a girl I could spend the rest of my life with.* The other girls were like my cars—fast and easy. Charlene was completely different. I could talk with her for hours about anything and I felt accepted by her. She also wasn't full of herself and she was very down to earth. She had a gentle demeanor, and I thought she was really good looking with her long hair. I was careful with her not to do a lot of preaching because I didn't want to drive her away if she wasn't ready. We just had regular conversations, and I prayed she could experience God as I had.

So I asked her out again and we went out to dinner. We had a great time and I couldn't imagine myself with any other girl. When I kissed her for the first time, it felt totally different than all the other kisses I had known. With the other girls there were no sparks, just a necessary prelude to something else. This time, with God in the equation, I had more than desire: I had passion with a desire for commitment.

Finally, after three months of dating, we started dancing around the issue of marriage. My dilemma was that I wanted her to experience the joy and peace I had so we could share that together. I knew this had to be the foundation of our marriage if it was going to work. But would she follow me in this new direction? That is what I had to find out.

CHAPTER 6
SHARING THE RIDE

Despite my apprehensions of losing Charlene I really didn't need to worry. The first time I dared to invite her to church she came. We sat down in a pew in the packed sanctuary and there was a feeling of expectancy from everyone who was there. As usual it was standing room only. The pastor led the worship with contemporary music and then gave a simple presentation of the gospel. I was praying silently that Charlene would be touched by the Lord, and when the pastor invited people to the altar to pray to receive Christ as Lord and Savior, Charlene did not hesitate. She just joined the flow of people going forward. When she returned to our pew she was beaming from the joy of the Lord and smiling from the excitement of what she had done.

So I met Charlene in November and she was born again in February. Right after her commitment to the Lord we both began attending services together. But then an event occurred that almost derailed our wedding plans. I had heard about this great restaurant in Ithaca called The Boxcar, and Char and I were going to take Bob and Wendy there to celebrate Bob's birthday. However, when I went over to Char's house her parents didn't want us to go because it was snowing heavily. I was set on going, so I discussed it with Char and we told them that we would take her car, which was a Ford station wagon. I figured it would be a little safer than my Camaro that still had summer tires on it. They still were not thrilled with the idea, but they could see we were going despite what they said. Of course, this action did not improve my standing with her parents and what happened later was even worse.

We ended up getting there with no problem and even on time for our reservation, but on the way home it was snowing more than when we left. Another driver ran a red light in Candor and we hit him broadside. Shortly after, we found out that the driver had more to drink than we did. In fact, he could hardly stand when he got out of his car and it wasn't from injuries. Everybody in our car just had bumps and bruises except me. I got the worst of it. I bounced my head off the windshield, the mirror and the roof of the car. Char's car was totaled on the spot. She then had the unpleasant duty of notifying her parents of our accident. When they arrived they were grateful that we were alive but not so happy with me. It would take years to get over that one. Of course, they made all of us go to the doctors the next day to get checked out. Everybody else was fine, but they insisted I check into the hospital because I had a concussion as well as neck and vertebrae damage. On top of that, after I went into the hospital they discovered that I also had mononucleosis.

Over the next ten days in the hospital I had a lot of time to reflect on the whole episode. The Lord convicted me right there of my drinking after that car accident. The Holy Spirit made it very clear, reminding me that I was DWI and they could have taken me away. I saw what people from my neighborhood went through who got DWI's and I had said it would never happen to me. In fact, I had the habit of slowing down when I drove under the influence. But I knew of many guys in my town who had wrecked their cars and lost their licenses. Some of them even got seriously injured or died. I kept thinking that if I had hit that guy one second earlier I probably would have killed him. I also thought maybe by a few seconds Char could have been killed, or Bob or Wendy. Lying on my white hospital sheets I knew I couldn't take that risk again. It was there I decided to abstain completely from drinking alcohol.

When I finally got out of the hospital I couldn't go back to work, because I was wearing a neck brace and was not allowed to pick up anything. Fortunately, I received some money from disability and the insurance company so I had some income. Despite the hardships, however, Char and I were still seeing one another, and I concluded if we were still going strong by May 1st I would ask her to marry me. I set May 1st as the date I would propose because it was my birthday and what better present if she agreed. I knew the type of ring she wanted, because we would often stop in front of jewelry stores and point to the ones we liked. Char liked the ring with the high-pronged setting in white gold with a diamond and so that's what I bought. That evening, when we went out on my birthday to our favorite restaurant, I offered it to a warm, receptive audience. We planned our wedding for September 9, 1972.

Even though I was excited about our big event, I was also pretty nervous. The Army draft lottery was taking place at the end of May and it could mean a radical change of clothes and location. They needed more soldiers for Viet Nam and the method was to put all the dates of the calendar in a lottery and then pick out the dates at random. The lower the number you had for your birthday the more likely that you would have to go in.

Some guys I knew decided to enlist rather than waiting and getting drafted. They falsely thought that they would have more of a say in what type of work they would have in the Army if they volunteered. My friend with the Corvette did that and signed up as a "tank mechanic," thinking that he would never be assigned to Viet Nam because there were no tanks over there. When they sent him there anyway he protested. They just agreed with him, "Yeah. You're right. There's no tanks over there, so you better carry a gun."

Although I prayed a lot about it, I was resigned to the fact that I would probably have to go in. All the guys I knew didn't resist, they just did their duty.

In the beginning of the Viet Nam War there was a marriage deferment to keep you from being drafted, but later it didn't make any difference. If you were a student you also had to maintain a certain average; if not you were thrown into the draft pool like everybody else. In my case, I had to go through the medical physical required for induction before the draft lottery. When I learned that my number was high I was ecstatic. That meant now I could get married without any worries.

Ironically, because the pastor at the Christian Missionary Alliance Church was not yet ordained, we asked the "old" pastor from the Methodist Church, whose church I attended rarely as a child, to do the ceremony. He readily agreed and we only offended people in two ways. One was not having the traditional wedding song, *Here Comes the Bride*, when Char walked down the aisle, and the other was suggesting that we have a "dry" reception. To the latter my family just said, "Well, you can forget about that." In both of our families we had relatives who were serious drinkers and my father's brothers alone probably kept several local bars in business.

I also realized as our marriage approached that I couldn't stay at the inn anymore. Even though the money was still good there, I knew I could not stay in that environment with the wild parties, guys cheating on their wives, and the drugs. For my own spiritual walk I knew I just had to quit and trust God to provide something better. When my dad found out that I needed work, he talked with his boss and offered me a job at his construction company. I ended up working with him on a school they were building in Pennsylvania for eight months.

Back in those days, construction jobs were a hazardous occupation. We didn't have the safety equipment that they have today and it was not uncommon to have a policeman at the work site because union workers would tend to get in fights with one another. In my youthful zeal I would even add to these risks. To give you an example, one time we were working forty feet in the air on six inch steel high beams. To make it less precarious they laid down two planks so I would have two feet instead of six inches of space to push my wheelbarrow full of bricks. But that wasn't fast enough for me, so I would just take shortcuts and veer off onto the six-inch girders. When the foreman saw me he went ballistic: "Hey kid! Whatta ya, outta your mind? There's men working underneath you. You drop one of those bricks and you're gonna kill somebody!"

But for some reason I did things like that frequently and the danger didn't faze me. I remember other times doing things just as risky, like going down 20 feet in a hole to cut concrete from a septic system. Those thousands of pounds of dirt could easily have caved in and crushed me, suffocating me within minutes. I didn't mind the risk taking, but as our wedding date drew near I purposely took fewer chances. One thing I didn't want to miss was my wedding day. I was so looking forward to it that I was even afraid that Jesus might come back before I could experience it. That was my mindset back then.

As a young Christian I shared my faith on the construction site, but not many of these rugged guys wanted to hear about it, especially from a young punk like me. But everybody has problems, and I found out when these guys were struggling with something they would often seek out the counsel of another Christian guy on the site who ran the heavy equipment. He was the first person to tell me about giving to the church. He pulled me aside one day and asked me, "Do you tithe?"

I said, "No, and I don't even know what that means."

"Well, that means giving 10% of what you make to the Lord. I now tithe 50% of what I make."

"You've got to be kidding."

"No. I live well. Got a new truck. A new house. God takes care of me. I give the Lord 50% and He blesses the other 50%. I lack for nothing and I'm happy."

I was pretty impressed by that. He had the respect of the other construction workers, too. It's funny, but one day a guy came up to this Christian while I was eating beside him and said, "You know I've got some problems with my wife and I wanted to talk to you about it." Then he looked over at me and said, "I know. I know.

Jesus is the answer."

When we got married we only had fifty dollars in our pockets. Our honeymoon consisted of two days in the Thousand Islands at the River Edge Hotel because we couldn't get the time off. I found a great apartment in Johnson City a couple of weeks before our wedding. The owner had converted a garage into three apartments and the rent was low. The only down side was that it was the scariest looking thing from the outside. It had been a two-car garage, and he made two apartments out of the bottom level and one apartment on top. So when you walked into this place it had concrete walls with old bricks with insulation hanging down from the ceiling. I remember taking people back there and watching them look up as if expecting to see rats jumping from block to block. The thing was, once you got through the rough-looking corridor and into the kitchen, it was really nice. He had done a great job. It was just the hallway coming in that looked like a dungeon. I think at the time it was costing us forty or fifty dollars a week.

The owner was a policeman from Johnson City; he didn't take any bull from anyone and he collected rent every Friday. I knew he wasn't a guy to be messed with when I saw him one day at an intersection in town literally pulling a guy out of his car and throwing him over the hood.

Fortunately, Char didn't have any trouble getting work near where we lived. She had gone to a two-year secretarial school in Binghamton and really knew her stuff. In fact, when the lady at Marine Midland in Binghamton gave her a long passage to type, she knocked it off so fast the lady came running back into the room to see if something was wrong. Char just smiled and said, "Everything's fine. I'm just done." She had typed the whole passage in record time and had zero mistakes; the lady hired her on the spot.

We also tried to find a church like the one we came from, but we couldn't find one. There was a CMA church a few doors down from our apartment, but although at first we thought that was great, we discovered rather quickly that the same dynamic was not there and we stopped going. Finally, we just gave up looking for a church locally and started driving all the way back to our former church in Owego.

Our first Christmas together I wanted to do something special for Char, so I bought her a red '64 Mustang convertible so she would have transportation to work. Later, I also bought myself a new SS Nova after my Camaro engine blew up. That was another fast car and I did a lot of drag racing with it, but that was something that was more my hobby; Char never really got into it.

The following spring of 1973 I had to find another job because the school project was finished. I collected unemployment for a couple weeks, until I couldn't take the inactivity anymore, and I found a mason's helper position that brought in only five dollars more per week than what I was making on unemployment. I just didn't like the feeling of being on the dole and being humiliated by the state workers interrogating me about how many places I had applied to for work that week.

The son of the owner was a nice guy, but the father was a bit of a tyrant. My job consisted of dragging heavy flagstone off a stonecutter and putting it on pallets. Some of these slabs weighed three hundred pounds and I would move them by myself. It got to the point where I was bulking up with so much muscle I could not even fit on our couch anymore to take a nap. It was like getting paid to pump iron all day and I probably haven't been in such good shape since. That job didn't last long though—probably only a month. I guess you could say that I quit and I got fired at the same time.

What caused it, however, was trivial. One day we were working out in the middle of nowhere and there was no place for a coffee break. Usually, we would be working in an urban setting and there was always some place to go. But here in the country there wasn't a coffee shop nearby so we didn't get a coffee break. Feeling cheated of our break, the rest of the crew and I decided to take the coffee break before work instead of later. Unfortunately, we didn't tell the owner what we were doing and we ended up arriving at the work site fifteen minutes late. He was not pleased with our tardiness and decided to dock us all an hour. To make up for the fifteen minutes that we lost he gave us the option of working until six o'clock. I told him that I had to leave at five anyway because I had to pick up my wife from work. By that time, we had figured out that Char's Mustang was costing us too much money, so we went back to only one vehicle. The owner, however, was not sympathetic and said, "You're fired!" I said, "No. I quit." I guess you could say it was a mutual separation.

But I wasn't concerned at all about not having a job. I knew that God would provide for us. Both Char and I were at peace about it even though some of our friends would ask us with anxious voices, "What are you going to do?" We would just say, "We don't know, but we know Who does." I knew one thing I didn't want to do was construction again. Although you were paid well because it was union work, the jobs were often inconsistent, and I didn't like dealing with all the layoffs or some of the characters like the mason.

After a while with nothing materializing, Char asked me, "So what are you going to do, Terry?"

I just said, "I'll just look in the paper and find something." So I got the paper, flipped to the classifieds, and there was a management position advertised for Kentucky Fried Chicken. I was thinking: *Well, how hard can that be?* I went for the interview and there were maybe six or seven guys there; only one other guy and I were in a suit and tie. Let me say this: the only two guys who got hired that day were both wearing suits.

It ended up being very convenient since my management training took place at the KFC in Johnson City, which was only about ten blocks from our apartment. Then my first job as an Assistant Manager was in Endwell, which was also really close— maybe five minutes away by car. From there they transferred me to a high volume store in Binghamton and that was only 15 minutes from our house. I felt really blessed by these transfers, because I was used to traveling 85 miles a day one way when I was working in construction.

At the end of six months I was looking forward to the opportunity of managing my own store. I was hoping it would be in the area, so I was surprised when the regional manager came up to me and said, "Terry, we've got a management position open in Syracuse. Would you consider taking this store?"

"I am definitely interested, but I'd like to check out the store first and the city." Believe it or not, I had never even visited Syracuse as an adult before, even though I only lived one hour away. But both Char and I were excited because we found a beautiful new apartment complex that we could afford and we liked the idea of living close to two lakes—Onondaga and Oneida.

The last thing to fall into place was Char's transfer to the Marine Midland Bank in Syracuse. This wasn't a problem because she got high recommendations from her former supervisors and they had an opening in the Trust department. She didn't even have to go for an interview.

CHAPTER 7
CHANGING LANES:
MOVING TO SYRACUSE

So we packed our bags and moved to Syracuse in the summer of 1973. Immediately, I started putting in 60-hour weeks, and sometimes even 90. The longest hours were the weeks just before store inspections. If the big wigs were coming to town, everything had to be ship shape.

Char was working two jobs: full-time at Marine Midland and part-time at Barbara Moss, a new women's clothing store at Penn Can Mall (now Driver's Village).

After we moved into our nice apartment on Bear Road in North Syracuse, we started looking for a church. We checked out the Missionary Alliance Church on Midland Avenue and the people were nice, but it just wasn't the same as the one in Owego. So, we did some church hopping for a while and then gave up.

I remember being particularly irritated by a sermon we heard at a Pentecostal church we attended. My mindset at the time was to excel and become wealthy. I was tired of being poor. Ever since working at the hotel restaurant I had made good money and had disposable income, so I stopped going to the church because of the pastor's view on money. I don't think what he said was necessarily wrong. It was probably more because of my sensitivity to the whole issue of money. I had grown up poor and I didn't want to repeat the experience. I also didn't agree with the philosophy that Christians should be poor and lacking in anything. I've always figured if I serve a God who created the universe, why should I lack anything? If I were the son of a senator, would I lack for anything? If I were the son of a millionaire, would I have to beg for the essentials? My philosophy was: If I am trusting in God and walking with Him to the best of my ability and I have a desire in my heart, it could very well come from God and He will grant it to me.

I have been amazed at all the times that God has given me the desires of my heart over the years. I have been blessed over and over again with things about which I have said in my heart, *I would like that some day*, and the Lord would present it to me later on down the road. It may not have been right away, but in many cases I would get it eventually. Sometimes I would have to put that desire on hold, but later it would come through with an even better deal than I had expected. In this instance, because of my spiritual immaturity, I let this sermon on money become a stumbling block in my walk with God, and I let church attendance slide in favor of working long hours and achieving the American dream.

At the same time I had a falling out with the district manager and went into the insurance business. The company was guaranteeing $500 per week as a minimum, selling insurance door to door. We would canvas different areas as a group during the week, and then if we missed someone, or someone owed us a premium, we would be required to go back on Saturday. Then Sunday we had to turn in our assignment and get our new one. Although I did make good money, it eventually became a seven-day-a-week job. I loved the idea of being my own boss. I could take time off because nobody was watching me, but I never did because I was on a roll, and when you're rolling it's hard to slow down.

It was a grueling schedule, and after a year and a half it began to wear on me. My priorities had subtly changed and now, instead of putting my spirituality first, I focused on getting ahead and making money. Sure, I still had my personal faith and I did the basics on my own like reading the Bible, praying, and sharing my faith: I just didn't see the need for the body of Christ at the time. I was young and still very independent. I just figured that I could handle everything on my own. In fact, my immediate supervisor was so impressed by my consistent numbers, he used to send out the new agents with me so they could learn how to sell.

But, to be honest, the job did have some serious drawbacks. It was not uncommon for people to sick their dogs on me or physically threaten me. One time as I was going door to door a man told me that he wasn't interested in what I was selling. The whole time I was talking with him, he was blocking his barking German shepherd from getting at me. When I turned around and started to leave, the dog bit me on the rear. Fortunately, I had a leather wallet in my back pocket so I was not injured. I reacted automatically and just swung around with my heavy leather binder and hit the dog in the head. He quickly yipped and scampered back to the door. I glared at his master while the man just smirked.

Another time I went to a local car dealership and asked the general manager if I could collect premiums from some of his employees. To me, he looked like a thug. He had black greasy hair, a black suit, and a stocky appearance. He looked at me and made a sarcastic comment: "Just get outta here or you'll be going to a one-car funeral."

I didn't quite get the drift of his comment but I knew it wasn't a compliment, so I replied with a taunt of my own. He responded by motioning to the two hefty salesmen next to him to escort me off the premises. When they were within about a yard of me I pulled back my suit jacket so they could see I was carrying a gun. Without losing a stride they both did a perfectly choreographed about face, and one of them said to the manager as he was passing him, "Why don't you do it?" He just looked stunned because he had not seen the gun. I figured now was a good time to leave on my own terms, so I just turned around and left.

It was incidents like these and the stress of working so many hours that made me wonder if it was all worth it. The final straw came when my district manager made a comment about a two-week period when I didn't produce as much as usual. He said: "Hey Bish. Your last couple of weeks have been kind of slow. What happened?"

I was surprised that he knew about that. Normally he never said anything—even when I had done extremely well. Now he was talking to me after I've had a poor performance. I was taken off guard. All I could come up with was: "Well, I've just had a couple bad weeks."

He responded, "You know what they say about shaving, don't you?"

I said, "No."

"If you miss two days of shaving you're a bum."

I determined right then to start looking for another job. I figured if all this company cared about was my production and nothing else, why should I stay? The following day I called an employment agency. I told them I wanted to make the same amount of money as I did with insurance but I didn't want to work so many hours. A few days later, the woman at the agency called me and said there were two positions open that did meet my criteria—one was selling stocks and bonds and the other one was working for a transmission shop franchise. I chose the latter.

Around this time, Char and I also took in my younger brother Rudy for a while. My mom called to tell me that she was thinking of leaving my dad, and Rudy was getting into so much trouble in high school she couldn't handle him anymore. She wanted to know if I could take him. I think my parents just grew apart from working so much—my mom now took care of two restaurants and my dad was still working long hours at construction. Rudy ended up staying with us his last two years of high school and graduated.

He soon discovered he couldn't get away with things with me that he could with mom and dad. I guess older brothers can sometimes have ways of persuasion that parents might be less inclined to utilize.

Working so much, of course, limited our social contacts and we developed few friends. Char had some friends at the bank and the store where she worked, and we would do some things occasionally with them and their spouses, but outside of that we saw very few people. There just weren't enough hours in the week.

I think my relationship with Char's parents got better since we didn't see one another quite so much; with my parents, however, things were rougher. They were going through hard times in their marriage, and it would spill out on me in the form of criticism of one thing or another.

When I started working for the transmission company, it opened a whole new world for me. I began attending seminars and reading the company's trade magazines. I would also go out and help the guys put in the transmissions so I knew how they did it, what the parts were, and how they functioned. By this method I got to know the business inside and out. My mechanical mind just seemed to absorb it very quickly. I think it helped, too, that I enjoyed expanding my knowledge. I also loved driving all the different kinds of cars like Jaguars and Mercedes. I loved, and still do, the feeling of getting behind the wheel of a well-made vehicle and seeing what it can do on the road.

I also made extra money on the side by buying a car, a snowmobile, or anything that I could fix and then selling it for a profit. It was around this time that Char and I got serious about buying a home, and we began to put money away for that purpose. After about two years we had saved enough. We wanted to buy an existing home, but at that time you needed ten percent down and that was a lot of money. Ryan Homes at that time was offering only five percent down for a new home, which was very reasonable. So we bought one in Brewerton for $33,000. It was the biggest three-bedroom house they made. It also had an oversized lot and was situated on a cul-de-sac, which made it very quiet.

When we moved into the new house in Brewerton, Char was pregnant with our first child. We had two children 19 months apart—Jonathon and Kimberly. We picked the name Jonathon because it was based on a great character in the Bible who was a loyal friend to King David, and Kimberly because we just liked the name. We were hoping for a boy and a girl in that order, and we were amazed when it really happened. We purposely waited five years after our marriage so we could enjoy our relationship and get more established financially. We were excited to become parents and felt it was the right time.

It wasn't long, however, before both of us were working full time again. I was still at the transmission shop and Char was working at a medical equipment manufacturer. She got a job there after Marine Midland scaled back and her office was closed. For me, it wasn't an easy time because it was the early eighties, and inflation and the interest rates were high (20% was the going rate). People were just plain angry and doing bizarre things. Some were even threatening me. One guy ripped his shirt off and punched a hole in the wall because he had just paid $500 to repair his three-speed automatic and he thought it should shift three times, not two. I had to explain to him that all three speeds only shift twice because you start out in first gear. Other people wanted to take me outside. The philosophy of this shop was to do everything fast and get it out within two days. This was when I learned about what they call "buyer's remorse" big time.

Char was also dealing with stress in a different way. She was working full time and taking care of two small children as well as the house. At this point, we were basically living for the weekend. I would be thinking about boating, hunting, or fishing and getting away from it all, and Char would be thinking of quiet times with the children.

But even when I was out on my adventures, it wasn't always that relaxing and I would sometimes find myself facing some unexpected challenges, especially when I was boating. Since the age of 14 boating has always been a part of my life. My first experience on the water was in Boy Scouts, when I learned to navigate a sailboat on Cayuga Lake. The adrenaline rush I felt sailing the boat on the point of near capsizing with the wind ripping through the sail and the waves breaking over the bow of the boat were a thrill like no other.

After I got married, however, I dropped sailing because Char didn't like all the leaning-over-the-side-of-the-boat action, so I got into motorboats when we moved to Brewerton. Starting with a 12-foot fiberglass Sears fishing boat powered by a 10-horse Mercury motor, I eventually upgraded to a 25-foot John Allman Sport Fisherman.

One of the amusing times with my first boat was when I went salmon fishing with my friend Bill on the Salmon River up near Pulaski. The method of fishing for salmon at this particular time was that fishermen would line up their boats on both sides of the river and then cast their trouble hooks toward one another. You'd reel in and yank until you snagged a salmon swimming up stream to spawn. During this season there are literally thousands of salmon going through and you had a good chance of getting a large salmon. Suddenly Billy snagged a big one. It took him off guard and pulled him out of his seat to the bottom of the boat three times before he was able to start reeling the fish in. A few minutes later I also snagged a large salmon and began reeling it in. By the time we both pulled them in, we noticed there was an unusual amount of water in the boat but we didn't think anything of it.

I put the two fish on a leader and threw it overboard. Thinking that the interior drain plug might not be fastened correctly, because the water kept coming in, I reached back to see if the latch was down and the whole plug just disintegrated in my hand. This, of course, made matters worse, and now the water came streaming in at a rapid rate. Usually, if you start up a boat the forward motion automatically drains the excess water out of the drain hole. In my haste I started up the engine, but I had forgotten to pull up the fish. The leader immediately got wrapped around the prop and the engine stalled. Now we were out in the center of the river with water still pouring into the boat. I quickly tipped up the motor so I could get at the leader better. It was difficult, because I had 50 pounds of salmon attached to the leader. The easier thing to do would have been just to cut the line, but I didn't want to lose our catch of the day.

Bill meanwhile was sitting in the front of the boat laughing at me. Apparently, it was not computing that he could be treading water in a matter of minutes. I ignored him and eventually untangled the mess and pulled the fish inside the boat. With the boat now half full with water, I started the motor and went back to the boat ramp to call it a day.

A couple of years later, Bill and I experienced a more harrowing experience on Lake Ontario. It was the day I went to pick up my Sport Fisherman. This boat was purchased from a man who lived on the St. Lawrence River who wanted to make an even trade for a motor home that I had used for weekend hunting, fishing and skiing excursions. He said, "I rarely use the boat, but I definitely will use the motor home."

My plan was to move the boat from the marina on the St. Lawrence River and then go across Lake Ontario and dock in Oswego. My friend Tom was going to meet us there for supper and then drive us back home. The following day Bill was going to drive Tom and me back to Oswego, and we were going to take the boat through the canal system to Brewerton. It was May 1st, my birthday, and I thought it was a great way to celebrate such an historic event. Little did I know how close this day would come to being the end date to a short life. I was 28 at the time.

It's funny how little decisions can have a major effect on future events. When we arrived at the dock where the boat was located, I saw right off that the compass was missing. Apparently the compass was a very expensive navigational device and the owner did not want to include it in our bargain—without telling me, of course. Compasses are vital, however, when you are boating in unfamiliar waters, so, despite the fact I was in a hurry to leave, I bought another one at the marina boat store. I also got some charts for the St. Lawrence River and Lake Ontario.

Just to show you how foolish I was, the only boats we saw out that day were huge tankers and they were moving fast—maybe 30 mph. Two of them were going in one direction and one was going in the other. My boat was supposed to go 50 mph, so I figured I'd just breeze past in between them. One of the trim tabs on the rear of the boat wasn't functioning properly, so at higher speeds it would lean to the left. To keep the boat a little more level I told Bill to stand on the right side of the boat.

As we were going by the tankers I was amazed at the immensity of the trough of water they were kicking out. The tankers must have been displacing thousands of tons of water, and it was as if we were in a valley of water with 15-foot walls on both sides. I also suddenly realized I had decided to pass at one of the narrowest sections of the river. At one point, above the wall of water, I could see guys from the tankers looking down on us. They probably couldn't believe what they were seeing and were coming to watch some crazy guys kill themselves.

Another thing that I didn't understand until later was how much silt and debris these powerful engines dredge up. We could easily have damaged our boat badly by being in their wake and hitting some tree stumps or worse as they were being dislodged from the bottom of the river.

Finally, we started across Lake Ontario. It was later than we had anticipated, because I had made a wrong turn into Canadian waters and the distance from the marina to Lake Ontario was farther than I thought. We also had to stop for fuel and we had to look for people to give us gas, because the marinas were not keeping regular hours. I had checked the weather and only two- to three-foot waves were predicted. *Piece of cake,* I thought. *A 25-foot boat shouldn't have problems with waves that size.* But what did they know? About half way to Oswego harbor we encountered eight-foot waves. These waves slammed hard against the hull and splashed as high as the fly bridge. Every time a wave hit the boat it was like someone pouring two pails of water on both of us. I was happy I had the compass at that point, because it was crucial that I knew the general direction we were going in. I also ran down below deck to see if the radio was working, just in case we needed to radio a "May Day" distress call. It was operational, but with the water at 40 degrees and no lifeboat, I knew we wouldn't last more than 30 minutes before we died of hypothermia if the boat went down.

Some guys told me later that nobody else was out on the lake that day because that early in the season there was often a lot of debris floating in Lake Ontario, and we're not talking pieces of dock but 60-foot trees and barn doors.

Meanwhile, Tom, who was going to meet us in Oswego, arrived at the destination and went to the Coast Guard station. When he didn't see us he thought he should let people know we were coming. The man at the station assured him: "Yes. We are well aware of the boat, "Pirate's Lady," and we are keeping a close watch on her." In fact, we had seen some planes go overhead and a Coast Guard boat along the way, but this did not reassure me, because I knew that it is almost impossible to find anybody in a sea with such large waves. I was glad, therefore, when I saw the power plant towers in Oswego as a reference point when we passed the half-way point. I looked at my compass and saw that we were only a few degrees to the east off course.

When we did finally arrive at the dock we were exhausted, saturated with water, but overjoyed to see our friend and to touch "terra firma." We walked squish-squash squish-squash into a restaurant, leaving a two-foot wide trail of water behind us, but we didn't care what people thought. We had deprived the lake of a few more victims and people's stares were nothing compared to being knocked around by the fierce waves. The management didn't seem concerned and let us stay. Tom said, "I was really worried about you. There's been zero visibility here all day. The fog just lifted before you came in."

Tom took us back to Brewerton and we came for the boat the next day. When I tried to start the boat, however, it just clicked like there was a starter problem. I checked out the starter and it just about fell apart in my hand. I informed Tom of the problem and he shook his head in disbelief. I went to the marina and they had exactly the starter we needed. After I installed it, it fired right up.

Then another amazing thing happened. We didn't go more than 100 yards upstream when the boat ran out of gas. I flipped the switch to the other gas tank and we were good to go. *What if that had happened while we were in the middle of the lake? I thought. We might never have made it. Would the starter have worked if we had run out of gas on the lake and then needed to start the engine again?* I shivered to think what could have happened. My revelations didn't stop here, though. Once we were through the lock and there was a wide open river, Tom said, "Hey, Terry, let's see how fast this thing can go. It's supposed to go 50 mph, right?"

Without needing any more encouragement I said, "All right, Tom, just hang on." Then I gunned it. The boat, however, started to veer to the right for some reason. The more input into the steering mechanism the less response I got. I finally had to shut the engine down and lift the engine hatch to see why I had no steering. If you are familiar with the Oswego lock, you know there is a set of falls not far from there. We were only a few hundred yards past the lock and now we were drifting back towards the falls. I was amazed to see that the brass coupling that held the steering mechanism together had cracked (probably from the violent beating the boat got on Lake Ontario) and the drift pin holding it had slid out. I looked around and found the pin and then taped it to the coupling so it wouldn't fall out again. Again I thought: *What are the odds that all these three things would happen in the span of 15 minutes? What if any one of them had happened during our crossing? We would have been at the mercy of the lake.*

The rest of trip down the canal was peaceful. We enjoyed passing through the little towns off the water and the colors of spring. When we reached the marina at Brewerton I backed the boat into my slip as though I'd been doing it all my life. It was nice to end such a treacherous journey on a positive note.

I just ran into Billy at a function recently and he still remembered the trip very clearly. He admitted that we could have died very easily that day. I realized, too, that I could have been swept overboard as I was going up and down the fly bridge ladder when those big waves were hitting us, but I wasn't.

Two years later I needed a new challenge, and I thought it was time to follow through on my interest in flying and get a pilot's license. I had started taking lessons in my late teens but stopped because of the cost and family responsibilities. Now that I was doing well financially I felt I could afford it, so I started flying out of Sair Aviation at Syracuse International Airport and took ground school at Onondaga Community College. A year and a half later I got my license. It was a great personal goal for me to follow through and do something I had dreamt of doing for so long. For me, flying is the ultimate adrenaline rush. There is no room for error in the air and you must multi-task constantly. You're required to talk to traffic control, fly the airplane, and be aware of what is in your air space as well as keep track of your heading.

While I was in the clouds, however, things were not going well on the ground. In the pursuit of adventure and personal achievements I had missed something essential in my role as a husband—my wife's needs. Charlene had taken another job with a refrigeration company and the people there began having a negative affect on her. They would go out together and drink, and they would invite her to go with them. I guess with my frequent absences she felt she wanted to have fun, too. This led to one of the most challenging and painful periods of our married life.

My first BB gun

Winning the buck contest

Boy Scout Camp

Left to right: Me, Jerry, Teena, Rudy

The fish I wouldn't let get away

25' John Allman before crossing Lake Ontario

Kimberly and Jonathon in front of our first house

Jonathon recovering from another leg injury

Jonathon making a comeback

Kim playing college soccer

Preflight inspection of 140 Cherokee Warrior

Dad gets tricked

Cessna 172: checking the fuel

The fastest pick-up truck Chevy ever made

The bear I almost left behind

*An Adirondack black bear cub
at six months*

Armed for bear

*Dad, I wanted a Corvette,
not a Corvair!*

*1969 Porsche 911: the car I sold
to start my business*

*BMW K1200 RS crossing the
Sunshine Bridge in Tampa*

Jaguar XKE Coupe

Still trying to make snowmobiles fly

Left: God stopped the snow

Below: And somebody said there wasn't enough snow!

Co-host John Metzler and I getting ready for "The Car Care Clinic" at 570 WSYR

Charlene and I with Glenn Beck on his tour bus after his book signing in Syracuse

Christmas with the family. L to R: Noah, Geoff, Kim, Me, Charlene, Jonathon, Zeke

CHAPTER 8
MISSING THE FLAGS: TIME FOR A PIT STOP

My routine would be to stop at our neighbor's house to pick up the kids after work. A next-door neighbor had kindly taken the responsibility of watching over them until I got home. More and more, however, I would get a call from Char after I got home saying, "I'm just going to stop for a bite to eat with friends from work," or "we're just going to listen to some music."

At first I figured it was only fair she got some space, too. After all, it wasn't unusual for me to tell her on the spur of the moment that I was going to take the boat out with some friends and not get home until late. I would do the same thing with hunting and sometimes even be gone for the whole weekend. Of course, I thought that she was just going out with the women from her job.

I was stunned, therefore, when a guy with whom I was lifting weights, and who worked at Char's company, told me: "Terry, you should be aware that there is a guy at my company who is making the moves on Char." The seriousness of it all became clear one day when I saw Char's car at a restaurant near where I worked. What troubled me was the fact it was already two o'clock in the afternoon. I had gone into the restaurant around noon and they said they were just having lunch. Now I saw their cars were still there while I was out on a road test. Well, this time I went in and I saw Char, and she was hammered and leaning on the guy I was warned about. When the guy saw me he moved away from her. All I could say was, "Char, you gotta go home."

I was wearing a gun inside my jacket, and to make my point I opened my coat so he could see my weapon, which was a 45 caliber Star PD. Once he made eye contact, I said, "For your own health, I would back off." I could see by the expression on his face that he took me seriously. I carried the gun because three managers a year on average got killed in our franchise nationwide by irate customers, and I didn't want to be added to the list.

Char verbally resisted going home with me at first, but she finally got up and went with me to the car. It was a quick, silent trip to the house but when we got there I tried reasoning with her about what just happened. She wasn't interested in talking and went into the bedroom to lie down. I was so mad I punched a hole through the bedroom door and returned to work.

The next morning she told me she wanted a divorce. The motive was simple: She was not happy with me and wanted out. I think she was just overwhelmed working full time, taking care of the house and kids, and putting up with an often absent husband and father. As she told me that, I felt immediately sick to my stomach and started to weep.

In the modern vernacular, I guess you could say I was pretty much a chauvinist. I didn't do anything in the house. I left the child-rearing to Char. I considered my role was just to be the breadwinner and I thought I was doing well. Meanwhile, Char was working full time, cooking, cleaning, taking care of the kids, and just getting burnt out. I figured I was doing my part if I just took care of the yard, the cars, and bought her what she wanted. I was in shock. In fact, when I looked at our neighbors, weren't we one of the few who actually had decent furniture in our house? I was making good money for that time period—around $35,000 a year plus the money I made on the side selling cars. We were both driving nice cars. We had a boat. We had a new house built.

I had heard there were two major reasons that lead to divorce. One was money and the other was a lack of communication. Since money couldn't be the reason, I quickly deduced it had to be communication. I never remember having fights about money, but we definitely had some major communication gaps. She didn't talk about things that bothered her, and many things I just didn't see. Thinking back, I know there were things I shouldn't have done and things I should have done. One thing I know I should not have done is bust on her about her weight. I don't know why I did this because she didn't have a weight problem at all. It was absurd. Yet I did it. I also should have given her more words of encouragement and less criticism.

I think a lot of my problem was just plain ignorance, and the rest was not having a real role model to show me how to love my wife. The only real life message I got from my dad about being a good husband and father was to work hard. In terms of communication my parents did a lot of yelling and fighting, but it seemed there was never any resolution of the problems.

Char was insistent, however, on getting a divorce, and I didn't know what to do. I even came up with an insane plan of both of us living in the same house, but living separate lives—for the sake of the kids, of course. Finally, I just said to her, "We really need to fix this thing, Char. I think you should go back home for a while . . . maybe for a week or two."

I had called her mom beforehand and told her that we had some issues to work through. I had explained what had happened and that I frankly did not know what to tell her daughter. I told her that Char wanted a divorce. Since her mother was always the disciplinarian in the family, I had confidence that she would know what to say. So Char packed up and went home and the kids stayed with me. They were probably five or six at the time. I also gave Char a picture of our family that she could take with her to remind her of us when she took her trips with the company. The company had a jet, and often she would be asked to fly to Alabama to the office down there for training.

I knew I had failed miserably in our marriage, but I also knew

I didn't want to lose Char, and I was willing to do whatever was necessary to keep us together. Char, however, had lost hope and I wondered if I was too late to make any difference.

CHAPTER 9
GETTING BACK ON TRACK

har was gone for about a week, which was about all she could take off from work. Meanwhile, I just couldn't get my head around the idea of getting divorced. I knew I loved Char. After all, we were Christians: How could this be happening to us? When I looked at our marriage I had thought things were fine. We didn't argue a lot. I saw enough of that while growing up that I didn't want to repeat the experience. Char, on the other hand, came from a non-fighting family, so she wasn't in the habit of arguing either. My parents also fought about money a lot, and Charlene and I never fought about that—we both had jobs and we were making more than the average. Yet, I was missing something big time.

When Char came back from her mom's she was still set on getting a divorce. I was confused about what to do. For the first couple of weeks we did not talk to each other. We basically just did our own thing. I had hurt her so badly, her sympathy for me was dried to the bone.

Finally, I got desperate and just went to the Assembly of God Church on Buckley Road and prayed. The door was open and no one was there, so I just went into the sanctuary and poured out my heart to God: *Lord, you see that Char wants a divorce, but I do love her and I don't really want one. I know I need to change. I don't want to lose Char. Please, help us not to get a divorce and help me to change. Amen.*

Not long after that Char came over to my work place for something, and before she pulled away I felt an urgency to go and just sit down in the car with her and share my heart.

"What do you think the Lord thinks about our behavior?" I started out. "He knows you've been hanging out in bars with your friends and I haven't been the best husband." Immediately I could tell my words had an effect. She suddenly looked sad and remorseful for what had happened and said simply, "I don't think He would be pleased with us."

I said, "Well, I want you to think about that for a while." She looked down but didn't respond. Although the arctic chill remained over the next couple of weeks, she did stop talking about a divorce. I also stopped going away all the time and began helping out with the kids and making her life a little easier. Finally, I told her that I understood some of her needs now and I asked her if she would give our marriage another try. She said coldly, "Okay, but it will never be the same." That remark hurt, but at least she said that she would try again, and I took that as a positive sign.

Gradually, things began to change. I started taking more of an interest in what she was doing. I stopped going away on the spur of the moment without her. I even started going shopping with her. I also started helping out more at home and giving her some space to do things with her friends. It was understood that when she did go out it was just with the girls and not the guys. I knew what I felt for Char was the real thing. I had had a lot of girlfriends in the past, but I had never met anyone with whom I wanted to spend my life. When I realized that there was a possibility of losing her after all we had experienced together, it really tore me up.

In the beginning it was rough. Although she had said she would give it a try, I could tell that her heart really wasn't into it and that she was still bitter and angry towards me. I tried not to dwell on that, and I persevered and made a conscious effort to change myself rather than looking for her to change first. In retrospect, I understand now that for a marriage relationship to grow and be healthy, you need to spend quality time together and communicate on a deeper level. I learned a lot of different lessons in marriage during this time of readjustment. For example, I learned that in general women need touch such as holding hands and hugs, not necessarily leading to sex. I also later understood if I wanted to have a better sex life I needed to help her with household tasks. This would lead to an expression of appreciation plus she wouldn't be so exhausted at the end of the day

In other words, the more I invested in helping her the more benefits I was reaping. The hard part during those initial months was not knowing where I stood in her life and if she was going to change her mind again and still want a divorce despite my best efforts. A turning point came at an unexpected time. We were both in the living room watching the sad news about the Challenger spaceship blowing up, and she spontaneously got up and came and sat on my lap. That was the first time she had shown me any affection for over a year, and I was happily surprised to see some visible sign of change in her heart towards me. It took us probably a year and a half, however, before we felt completely comfortable around each other again. She had to work through her feelings of being hurt and resentful, and I had to deal with my feelings of being betrayed.

CHAPTER 10
TAKING THE WHEEL
AND FLYING SOLO

As our family grew and our financial responsibilities increased, I asked the owner of the transmission shop for a raise. He just said, "I can't pay you any more than what I am paying you, and I could hire someone ten years younger for $10,000 less and he would be thrilled at the offer."

Seeing that my prospects at this shop had reached a plateau, it was clear that my time there was limited. And, as strange as it sounds, I decided in 1987, during that time of emotional upheaval and uncertainty, to quit my job at the transmission shop and start my own repair shop. I had saved up $10,000 and I also had a Porsche, which I sold for another ten grand, so I had $20,000 to invest in a business.

An unexpected opportunity arose when a guy who sold radiators told me that he wanted to sell his business. He explained that his father had built a successful radiator business over the years, but after he retired and handed it over to him, he discovered that he was more interested in real estate than radiators. So I bought his business for ten grand and rented the building from him with the stipulation that I could purchase the property after two years. It was basically a turnkey operation. He had been making a couple grand a week by himself with just selling radiators. He had no interest in working on cars. All he wanted to do was sell radiators over the counter.

To give you an idea where Char and I were at the time, she took off to visit some friends in Michigan on my shop's opening day. I don't think she cared one way or the other about the new business. In fact, my parents came up from Owego and helped me organize and get the shop ready for customers. I was disappointed that she wasn't there, but I also knew I couldn't stop her from seeing her friends. She probably figured that this was just another thing that Terry wanted to do, and once he got something in his head there was no stopping him. I've since come to the conclusion that this trait is just a part of my personality and is a positive thing as long as I don't let it get out of control.

At that time the radiator business was protected and if anyone—and that included garages and service stations—needed a radiator they had to go to a radiator shop. When I took over, I decided to expand the business by not only selling the radiators but also installing them and doing anything else related to the cooling system. In a short time the shop went from a couple thousand a week to five or six thousand a week. I did that by myself for five months until I saw I could not keep up with all the work, so I hired an employee. Within a couple of months I hired my second worker, who could rebuild transmissions as well.

I believe it was purely the grace of God that led me to that opportunity at that time. With only 20 thousand dollars to invest and not having a name for myself in the field, it usually would have taken a lot more time to build up a business. I just happened to walk into an ideal situation with an established business at a reasonable price and the bright idea to expand on an already profitable enterprise. I decided to call it *Terry's* because a lot of people knew me from the other company.

I felt people trusted me over there because I refused to get into shady practices and would also fix things for free if it was just a simple adjustment somewhere. I figured there were plenty of car problems out there to keep me going honestly and if there weren't I had better find another kind of business fast. I did give people the option of getting a lifetime guarantee, but I would not tell them they needed an overhaul if only the vacuum line was off or the linkage was out of adjustment.

Previously I had tried to buy a franchise from the company I had worked for and had even gone to Ithaca for a year to prepare for the transition, but we couldn't work out the details and what they were asking was beyond my capability. When the time stretched to a year and there was no sign of anything changing, I had returned to my previous location in Syracuse. It was seven years before the radiator business opened up. I think I was just getting ahead of God's timing for me. Yes, He did want me to have my own business: It just wasn't through this franchise.

After three years, *Terry's Transmission / Bill's Radiator* did so well I bought another business down the road, which was doing heavy truck and general repair. The owner was going through a nasty divorce and offered to sell me his company and his property at a reasonable price, and he was willing to hold the mortgage. Eventually, however, I discovered that it was just too difficult to run two locations at the same time. I also saw that the heavy truck side of the business was not cost effective and I discontinued it. I decided that it would be better to move the transmission and radiator business into our new location and rent out the other property.

Years were going by and our marriage was definitely better, but I knew it was still not what it should be. I thought about going back to church, but now the children were heavily into soccer and, of course, the games took place on Sundays, so the thoughts came and they went until we were . . . blindsided.

CHAPTER 11
BLINDSIDED

I t was New Year's Eve, 1992, and Char and I decided we didn't
want to go the party route this year. We wanted a low-key cele-
bration so we just went to a movie with the kids. Jonathon was
14 and Kimberly was 13. I don't remember the name of the movie,
but what followed it I'll remember for the rest of my life. As we
walked out of the movie theater my son suddenly said,

"Hey, Dad. I don't feel so good."

"What's wrong?"

"I feel like I have the flu. I feel achy and hot all over."

We all stopped walking, and I put my hand on his forehead
and it was warm. Of course, I was thinking: *Great! It's New Year's
Eve. We want to have a good time as a family and now he's sick.*
When we got home Char took his temperature and it was confirmed: He had a fever.

On New Year's Day, however, he was not doing better, and now
he was feeling really sick. He also kept complaining about his leg.
I told him to show it to me and he rolled up his pant leg. What I
saw was this big red blotch going down his leg. I knew a little about
infections from Boy Scouts and this looked serious, so I called up
the Emergency Room. The doctor on duty said, "I think you are
being a little over concerned." I argued with him for about five
minutes because that redness to me meant it was infected. He also
had a high temperature. Finally, the doctor said, "Oh, okay. Why

don't you bring him down and we'll take a look at him."

When we got to the ER the doctor came over and examined my son's leg and I could see he was immediately concerned. I couldn't help it and I blurted out, "I was talking to this bonehead on the phone and he didn't think it was any big deal."

The doctor turned towards me and said, "I was the bonehead you were talking to."

Obviously after seeing Jonathon he changed his mind and had him admitted right away for emergency surgery. What made it worse was that the doctors did not tell us what kind of infection it was or what they were doing. Every time he started to feel better it seemed they wanted to do another operation because they weren't happy with what they saw. His wound also was getting bigger and bigger after every surgical procedure. Finally he was diagnosed with a bone infection, and they started giving him morphine because the pain was so bad.

By the third operation in the third week we asked my friend Billy's wife, Bethany, who was a nurse, what she thought. After hearing everything about the wound and what the doctors were doing, she instructed me to pose certain questions in medical terminology to the physicians. When I did the doctors confessed: "Yes, it is very serious and he may die. We honestly do not know what is causing the infection. It may be time to call in a specialist."

They then called Upstate Hospital and were put into contact with a woman who was an Infectious Disease Specialist. Immediately she came in and started taking cultures from his leg so she could experiment with different possible solutions. Within a week she told us she had found a concoction that could kill the bacteria, but it came with a warning: "Yes, I did come up with something that is killing the bacteria, but you need to know there are some risks involved. It could cause heart failure or damage, and it could even collapse his valves. He also could lose his hearing."

And this was just a partial list of all the negative things this "concoction" could do to our teenage son. Yet, at the same time, this "concoction" could also possibly save his life and his leg. We were convinced we had to take the risk.

She went on to say, "We'll have to transport him back and forth to Upstate and start running tests on his heart valves as we administer this stuff, because he could have a heart attack."

At this point we were terrified and prayed constantly to God to heal our son and to give us peace in the midst of the trial. Our son was totally out of it most of the time, which made it doubly hard since we could not really communicate with him. The morphine made him hallucinate, and he was on it for so long that they had to keep upping the doses, so we feared, on top of everything else, that there might be other adverse effects. At the end of four weeks they still didn't know if he would live or die, and there was a possibility that they might have to amputate his leg.

Meanwhile, my business had grown so much by then that I had to hire a manager and a dozen guys to keep up with all the work. Char had also come to work with me. Her former employer had pulled up stakes and moved out of Syracuse, so it was a logical step for her to put her administrative skills to work at *Terry's*. I can only give God thanks that He held it all together when I sometimes didn't know if I was coming or going.

The physical effects on Jonathon were minimal considering all the serious things the specialist had said might happen. Out of the whole ordeal he lost some hair, had a badly marred-looking leg, and endured two more operations. The doctor explained to me that the wound was so wide they couldn't close it, so they had to take muscle from the other side of his leg and stretch it around to the front and do skin grafts to close it up. Jonathon ended up being in the hospital for eight weeks.

The doctors told us that the way the bone healed was completely out of the ordinary. What really surprised them was the way the bone had grown back on the backside of his leg. In fact, they said they had never seen it happen before—the bone on the backside of his leg had actually grown another layer over the old bone as if reinforcing it. The medical bill of $60,000 was astronomical, but we fortunately had health insurance that covered the whole amount minus the deductible. Jonathon didn't miss a beat in soccer, and went on to play in high school, and Herkimer Community College where they won the national championship.

After making it through this life and death struggle, Char and I did not want to just slip back into the old ways of doing things. We had recommitted our lives to the Lord during this time and we wanted to honor that commitment. It wasn't until my son got seriously sick that we began to examine our lives a little bit and do some soul searching. Then we realized that a lot of our relationship with the Lord was based on convenience—what was convenient for us. We knew this had to change.

CHAPTER 12
FINDING A NEW PIT CREW

After Jonathon was healed, Char and I got serious about walking with God, and we cleaned all the stuff out of our lives that had crept in over the years. We poured all the alcohol in the house down the drain, because we felt that God wanted us to get radical about doing a complete housecleaning. For us, we felt it was just too much a part of our old lives to keep the bottles lying around. I also found some porn videos that I had in my closet that I had bought from my former boss, and we destroyed those.

We also got serious about finding a local church, and we finally decided on the Brewerton Assembly of God. We had visited the church several years earlier when they were meeting in a furniture store, and by 1991 they had grown so much that they already had their own building. The pastor reminded us of the preacher at the Christian Missionary Alliance Church in Owego, who had led both of us to the Lord, so we immediately felt welcomed. We also sensed the presence of the Lord there, and we were excited about getting involved. I knew God could do miracles and I started seeing it happen. I saw people laying their hands on other people and praying for them, and then seeing them healed of cancer or delivered from financial disaster.

I saw God come through with my business so many times, too. We would be walking on the edge financially and then the Lord would always provide work in the nick of time, or we would receive money from an unexpected source.

Going to church, however, was a tough transition for the kids because regular church attendance had never been part of their lives. They were used to playing soccer or other sports on Sunday with their friends, and now they had to go to youth group where they didn't really know anyone. Teenage years are an awkward stage anyway, and I guess they felt that we had just compounded the difficulty.

As our kids continued in the youth group, they both accepted the Lord somewhere down the line. I saw my daughter Kimberly as someone who was more prone to walk the walk. Kim was the type who knew what she wanted in life. Her career track started as early as twelve years old when she overheard how much her braces cost. She just put two and two together, and figured out that the people in that field were making good money and it was a worthy goal to pursue. The funny thing was that she never deviated from that vision, and when she graduated from high school she found a college that had a dental hygienist program, received her degree with high honors and was offered a great position at a local dental office.

School, however, was not easy for her. She had to study hard for good grades, but she got them. Whatever she did she was (is) disciplined, whether it be academics, sports, or morals. I was particularly impressed as her dad when she was 16 and came home early one night because she didn't want to follow her peers to a beer party. I wasn't even aware of this until the father of one of her friends knocked on our door and asked if Kimberly knew where his daughter was. I called her to the door and explained why the man was there. She said, "I do know but I would rather not tell."

"You better tell him, Kim. He needs to know," I insisted.

She did not hesitate: "She went with the others to party at Panther Lake."

I can't express how proud I was that she stuck to her principles when I am sure all her friends were pressuring her to go.

Jonathan, on the other hand, got involved with the wrong crowd and went in the opposite direction, as I had done. The negative side of his superior athletic ability was that it got him on the varsity soccer team when he was younger, and he just joined in with whatever the older players were doing. He was a big kid and he later got a reputation of being a "mean dude" who worked as a bouncer at bars. He was known as someone who could knock people out with one punch, and he was not afraid of getting physical with someone. It was hard for Char and me to see him going the same route I had gone, but we believed if God could save us He could also save our son. We just persevered in prayer and tried to keep the lines of communication open. Actually, it was just recently that he got baptized and he is now a member of our present church, Abundant Life, but that's his story, not mine.

Going back to church, I discovered how selfish I had been. For years, even though I had faith in God, everything revolved around me—what I wanted, what I wanted to do. Yet, an essential thing was missing—applying the "one another" passages in the Bible to my life. Serve "one another." Bear "one another's" burdens. Pray for "one another." Love "one another." Now that we were back in church, I could do those things regularly instead of only occasionally. I attended prayer meetings where I could pray for others and they could pray for me. I committed myself to go to Bible studies where I could hear the word of God and become stronger spiritually and in my witness for Christ. In short, I found out that I needed other people in my life and that I didn't do well as an island. The other amazing thing was they also needed me and what I had to offer.

I know getting plugged into a church as a man is especially hard. I've been there, done that. We've been brainwashed to think that we have to be self-sufficient and independent, needing nobody, when just the opposite is true. The fact is, men need close relationships with other men—not just for playing golf with, but in order to grow spiritually. We need more mature men in the faith to mentor us or hold us accountable to biblical standards because, let's face it, we need other men to help us stay sharp spiritually. In other words, "iron sharpens iron." We weren't meant to do this thing called life on our own.

It was really after Char and I started giving of ourselves to the Lord and serving others that we began to see our business grow, our relationships prosper, and our children also being touched by the Lord. I firmly believe that the Lord has that kind of life for all of us. He wants to bless us in so many different ways, but we cannot shut ourselves off from Him or other people, because that can limit what He can do.

I found out, too, that as I was faithful in the little tasks I was asked to do in the church, I was given the opportunity to serve in more responsible positions, such as the church council. Here I was asked to give my input on various church issues, whether they were spiritually related or having to do with some business aspect of the church. Years later I was asked to lead the men's ministry. I was thrilled to share with the men some of the lessons I had learned about family relationships as well as providing social events where we could build relationships together.

In the men's ministry, we also looked at ways we could improve our marriages and the way we related to our children. For example, I saw in my own life and in the lives of a lot of other dads the tendency to be quick to criticize our kids and to say "no," and slow on the compliments or even slower on the praise.

I shared with the men's group how I had to change the kids' image of me from "Dad the Enforcer" to "Dad the Builderupper." As in many families, Char would sometimes say to the kids when they were disobedient: "Wait until your father gets home!" Although that was sometimes effective in getting them to change their tune, it also gave them the primary perception of me as "Mr. Discipline." I knew this had to change so I started to encourage them more on things they had done, even if it seemed like a small accomplishment. I think this, more than anything else, helped them to respect me more and be more willing to listen to me when I asked them to do or not to do something. I also saw that this gave them self-confidence and a positive self-esteem.

I was glad that God could use this and other experiences in my life to help other men. I have included a powerful story at the end of the book in which God came through in a big way during one of these men's ministry times, and one man's life was radically changed as a result.

I've found that every day I have an opportunity to affect people either positively or negatively through my words and actions. One of the things that has helped me quiet my mind and heart over the years has been to go hunting and spending a lot of time with nature. Normally it takes me at least two or three days to get all the clutter out of my mind and enjoy the serenity of my surroundings. Then I start to ask God about things and listen to His still soft voice in my heart.

I remember one particular time I was having difficulty knowing what to do about my business. I wanted to buy the building we were renting, and I just couldn't figure out how I could get enough money together to do it. As I walked in the woods and waited on God, a thought came to my mind about the contract I had signed that I had completely forgotten about. *Your contract states that as you were paying the rent a percentage of that could be applied to purchasing the building.* The answer was right in front of me but I didn't know it until that moment. The total came to exactly what I needed to buy the building.

CHAPTER 13

OFF THE TRACK: HUNTING STORIES

As I stated earlier in the book I've always spent a lot of time in the woods. Whether it was hunting, trapping, fishing or something else, I just loved being in the wild. By the age of ten I was probably already staying out in the forest all day by myself, just tramping around. Sometimes it was with my brother Jerry. I know today parents would probably be horrified not to know where their children are for so long, but back then there was little talk about child abductions and sexual predators, so people, especially in the country, often let their kids roam free. In my case, my parents probably couldn't afford the luxury of worrying because they were just too busy working and trying to make ends meet.

I started hunting birds and rabbits when I was nine years old, after my grandfather gave me a BB gun. Later, when I was 12, he gave me my first .22. I went through the hunter's course as soon as they let me. I've got a photo of me holding that BB gun and it looks twice as tall as I am. I still have the .22 also, and it still looks brand new.

Nobody ever took me out hunting, even though most of my uncles hunted regularly. I just learned it on my own. When hunting season came around, as I mentioned earlier, I skipped school every Monday and hunted whatever was in season. My parents didn't know about it but the school authorities did, and one time in high school I had to go to summer school because I had missed so many days.

One of the funniest things I liked to hunt was duck. I still have memories of a whole line of hunters of various ages on the shores of the Susquehanna River, waiting for the ducks to come cruising in at 60 mph. As they approached you could hear everybody shooting at them and it just got louder the closer they came. Everybody could tell where I was positioned because I was the only one shooting a 10-gauge shotgun while the rest shot 12 gauges. My 10-gauge was heavy, close to 15 pounds. To give you an idea of what kind of gun it was, they used to use the old 10-gauge slug to shoot elephants. You'd hear their guns: bam, bam, bam, bam and then mine: BOOM! The reason I preferred the 10-gauge was for the distance. When you were shooting ducks and geese high up in the sky you had to have something that could reach them.

Ducks, I learned, were pretty much brainless. You could have a barrage of hunters shooting at them, and they would fly right through the rain of fire instead of flying higher out of danger. When a group of ducks flew into our area we would probably take down over half of them. What really got us laughing and rolling on the ground when I was a teenager, of course, was when we would use a duck call and the ducks would come flying right back to the same place where we had just mowed them down.

I remember one time when I was 16 I shot a duck and it fell down into the Susquehanna River in Owego. I didn't have a dog to do the dirty work for me, so I thought I would just swim out and get the duck myself. It was in the fall and I learned something I will never forget—good swimmers can drown if the water is cold enough. Their muscles just freeze up and don't function anymore. And that is exactly what happened to me. After I picked up the duck I started swimming back to shore, but as I did I lost all feeling in my arms and legs. I couldn't believe it. I couldn't move forward and I started to sink down in the water. The only thing I could think of to do was to arch my back to try to straighten up. That brought me to an upright position, and my feet landed flat on the bottom of the river. Fortunately, it wasn't that deep so my chin was just barely out of the water. I then realized that I was able to move my thighs, so I just pushed forward until the water level dropped to my chest and then to my waist and then low enough so I could walk out of the water.

I now understand what happens when the body heat drops below a certain level. At a certain temperature the muscles shut down. When I hear about people jumping in Green Lakes and drowning, even when they are expert swimmers, I know it is because of this phenomenon, not because they are not strong physically. The water is just too cold. People get fooled when it is hot outside but cold underneath the surface, where it hasn't warmed up yet. If the water is 40 degrees you can die. The sensation is not painful, but once you lose control of your limbs, you've just lost your ticket out—unless it is shallow water, as in my case.

One event marked me forever when it comes to hunting geese. I was out hunting ducks when I saw this lone goose flying around at low levels, obviously looking for its mate that had been shot. It was one of the saddest things I have ever witnessed in nature. It was honking this really mournful sound, and I knew it was in anguish over the loss of its companion. I knew that geese mate for life and I just watched it. It didn't care how low it was or what it sounded like. It got so close to me I could have just killed it in an instant, but I couldn't do it. I had heard the sounds of geese in a lot of different situations, but I had never heard anything as forlorn as that goose honking. I figured if geese have the sense to mate for life, maybe they are not as dumb as we think. I never hunted geese again after that experience.

One of the places I loved to hunt was up in the Adirondacks. Sometimes I would go with Jerry or friends, but many times I would just take off for two or three days at a time and sleep in my car or truck and then hunt during the day. One time I even went deer hunting in my Corvette to Binghamton and came home with a six-point buck on my trunk.

I can't say I've ever shot a bear, but I've come close. I've also chased a few. One thing I didn't want to do is stoop to killing "dump" bears, which were bears that liked to go to the dumps to eat. Some hunters would just wait on the trail to the dump and nail them on their way to lunch. I wasn't very inspired by this type of hunt, because number one it was illegal and number two the bears that were shot at the dump always looked to me like they were unhealthy and had gnarly fur. Since my goal in bear hunting wasn't for the meat (which isn't good tasting in my opinion) but for the fur, I wanted healthy bears that preferred a natural diet.

Therefore, I would go looking for bears where there were a lot of berries or caves. I could see where they went, because at times the brush was so dense they had to burrow. I would even get down on my hands and knees and go after them. Sometimes I got so close I could hear them grunting and snarling ahead of me, trying to get away. I chased three of them one day, trying to get close enough to get a shot. I was not overly concerned about those bears turning around and attacking me, because I knew that bears generally are very skittish and afraid of humans. So I just kept pursuing them through the brush. Little did I know that at that moment another hunter just walked into the woods. He was not ten feet into the woods when the bears came rushing right at him. He shot one of them in the head and downed it immediately while the others ran in separate directions.

Another time I went bear hunting with Jerry and I found an ideal spot to wait for them. I saw bear tracks coming up from the swamp and I told Jerry, "This looks like a good area. Let's just sit and wait and pretty soon some other hunters will push them right into us." Sure enough, a short time later, two guys came into the swamp and drove these two bears right up the hill where we were waiting. Before we could shoot them, though, a guy stepped out of the woods from the other side of the trail and shot one. The other bear turned around and was heading back toward the swamp when one of the guys who was pushing them shot that one. So I have never bagged a bear, but I've seen three of them taken.

I know a lot of people are really fearful of bears, but the truth of the matter is they are more afraid of you. Of course, if you wound one or get it cornered, or you get between a mother and her cubs, you could have some serious problems, but for the most part wild animals are quick to flee when humans approach. In all the reading I've done over the years about bears, they say that the most dangerous age of bear to watch out for is the age just before they are fully mature—or in the 250 pound range. For whatever reason these bears are more aggressive toward humans. When you hear about a black bear killing or maiming someone, nine times out of ten it is this teenager bear or a wounded bear that has done it.

To be honest, sometimes you need to be more concerned about getting shot by other hunters than being attacked by an animal. That is why I like to go to the Adirondacks. The area is so vast, and if you go far enough out you generally won't meet anyone else. Many hunters like to hunt right off the main trail. I guess they figure if they do get something it will be easier to drag it a short distance.

I like to go 10 plus miles back where it is very easy to come across a deer or a bear because they are not used to seeing humans that far back in the woods. My goal in hunting is always to try to kill the animal on the first shot. This is a real challenge when there is dense brush. One thing I never want to do is to maim an animal. If I don't think I have 100% chance of killing it in one shot I don't shoot. I've hunted with many different types of weapons—everything from a .30-06 rifle to a .44 Magnum handgun as well as a bow and arrow. I used to be pretty accurate with a 75-pound recurve bow and I could put three arrows into a deck of cards from 45 yards out. I've taken almost every kind of game with the bow and arrow in upstate New York, including foxes, rabbits, deer, and squirrels.

When I trek back into the Adirondacks, I make sure I take a compass, a backpack with food, a first aid kit, and a couple of hundred extra rounds of .22s. I always carry a .22 with me for two reasons. One, it is easier to carry a couple of hundred rounds of ammunition for a .22 than for a shotgun. Also, I figure if I injure myself or get lost and am out there for days, the gun is small enough caliber so I can hunt for rabbit or squirrel and at least feed myself while I am trying to get back out. Of course, today this is not as relevant as it used to be due to handheld GPS's and cell phones.

I am pretty good with a compass so I'm not afraid of getting lost in the woods. I learned how to use one in Boy Scouts. We used to have a lot of compass reading competitions and I always enjoyed that. Only one time do I remember thinking something was wrong, because I didn't see a main trail that should have been there by my calculations. I finally figured out that the reason I didn't see it was because of all the brush that was blocking my view. Still, I was only ten yards away from where I should have been. I also like to carry ropes with me because I find that I can save myself a lot of time on a hunt sometimes if I just rappel down a bluff instead of walking another half mile to find a way down.

Trying to Get a Bead on the Bouncing Buck

One time I was deer hunting with my friend Skip behind my camp in the Adirondacks. Since we were on a mountainside, I sent Skip down to the bottom and I said I would try to push any deer to him. As I started down the mountain I came across a fresh buck scrape and deer tracks. A buck scrape is a section of ground that has been cleared away by the buck in hopes that a doe will urinate in the dirt, so he can smell the scent and then pursue her for mating purposes.

Knowing the buck was near, I slowed my pace and began to survey the landscape for any movement or any color that would indicate a deer. I could tell this was a big deer because the tracks went between trees that were farther apart, revealing that it probably had a wide rack. Suddenly, I caught a glimpse of brown fur moving through the green pines, and he turned and saw me at the same time. I saw then that he had a rack of at least eight to ten points. I expected him to run down the mountain towards Skip, but instead he turned towards the 100-foot cliff and leaped into oblivion. I couldn't believe it. The buck must have known Skip was waiting for him further down because he didn't hesitate to leap. I thought for sure he had killed himself, but when I looked down over the precipice I saw him hit a rock that was sticking out and then bounce to another bluff and then jump all the way to the ground. This deer was a champion: Each jump must have been 25 feet. I couldn't even rappel down there because I didn't have my ropes with me. We weren't really far from my camp and I didn't anticipate needing them. But the deer had no fear. He just threw himself off the ledge and hit those different rock protrusions like he had it all planned.

Once he hit bottom he ran further into the woods, but he did throw a glance in my direction to see if I could top that act. I couldn't. I had to go another 200 yards just to find a place where I could somewhat safely slide down an embankment so I could chase him. At this point I forgot about Skip and was thoroughly into the hunt. Poor Skip never saw him.

In hunting there is a method of running deer down. Now deer are fast, but they don't have much endurance, so although you cannot outrun a deer in the short distance as a hunter, you can definitely outrun a deer if you persevere. That is why dogs can also catch a deer. They just keep running until the deer is exhausted and cannot run any longer.

I knew that fact, so I kept chasing the bouncing buck over some open woods and then through a swampy area. There I even had to walk in water up to my waist carrying my .30-06 rifle over my head. I kept following the tracks and I could see he was getting winded. I saw he was running and not making long bounds like before. His tracks showed as well that he was starting to tire, because he was dragging his hooves in the snow. I got occasional glimpses of him through the brush and trees, but I couldn't get a clear shot.

Finally, he moved into some heavy pines and on the other side he joined a small herd of six deer. Within a minute or two they formed a circle and then they all ran out in six different directions. Deer are smarter than you think, and what they did was a tactic to try and confuse me by bounding out randomly like that.

I examined the different hoof prints by walking in a circle and moving outward until I found the tracks of my deer. It wasn't too difficult because all the other tracks showed deer bounding great distances. Only one set of tracks revealed a deer that just bounded a short distance and then began dragging its hooves. By this time I had been chasing this buck for about forty-five minutes. I knew I had to get him soon or else give up the hunt. I was just too far off the trail and Skip was still waiting for me at the bottom of the mountain.

As I tried to quicken my pace to catch up with the buck, I could see another mountain cliff coming up. I figured I had him, but I was wrong. Somehow that tired, muscular buck zigzagged up that steep grade and made it all the way up to the top. All I could do was shake my head and stare up the escarpment in amazement. There was no way I could climb that cliff. He had beaten me fair and square and he deserved his freedom. I let him go.

Bear Hunting in Northern Canada

My bear-hunting trip to northern Canada came about in an unusual way. I attended the RV trade show at the NYS fairgrounds in Syracuse, and I met this guy named Danny who had a booth next to mine. I was promoting our transmission and radiator business, and Danny was promoting his father's two RV dealerships. We were about the same age and he too had a passion for hunting and camping. During our discussion I told him that I was looking for a conversion van, and he said to give his father a call at his dealership down in Florida when we arrived. I was planning to go down there in the spring to visit my parents anyway, so I looked up his brother and bought a beautiful Ford E150 High Top Conversion Van. A month later Danny called me and invited me to go bear hunting with him and some of his friends in September in northern Canada. One of the guys in his group had backed out and he wondered if I wanted to take his place.

I had never shot a bear or hunted in Canada before, so I readily agreed. I also thought it would be a great opportunity to try out the van, so I volunteered to drive.

The place they wanted to hunt was so far north that the roads stopped before we arrived at our final destination. After the roads ended, we had to take the train that went through the Canadian mountains. We had to bring everything with us because we would be far from civilization. If we really needed anything, we would have to check the train schedule they gave us and make sure we were near the tracks when it came by. When the train screeched to a halt, we then had to give our list to the conductor, who would pick the stuff up for us and then deliver it the next time he came through.

Once we were dropped off at the appropriate spot in the middle of nowhere, a guide met us with a four-wheeler and a little trailer attached, and took us and our gear to a river that was 15 minutes away. At this location there were three motorboats where we loaded in all our equipment and food supplies, and then he led us for another 15 minutes to the campsite. The base camp was a two-story log cabin with no electricity or running water. It had a wood-burning stove that was used for both heat and cooking. There were three beds upstairs and a fold out couch bed downstairs. After we unloaded everything, the guide said he was going to show us the four baited sites for the bears.

When he showed us the first site I said, "This is the site I would like." He asked, "Why do you want this one?"

"Based on my experience of bear hunting in the Adirondack Mountains, I know this site would be an excellent spot because of the type of vegetation that's here, the swamp is good cover, and the trees come right down to the water's edge."

"You're right. This is the best site, but our tradition is to draw straws for the sites."

Unfortunately, I pulled the straw for the baiting site the farthest out, and Danny from the trade show got the best site. He ended up getting a bear the first night and becoming the camp cook. To get to my site I had to get in a boat and cross the lake, get into another boat and go about a half mile and get out, and then take a third boat and go up another lake. In all it probably took me forty-five minutes just to get to my site.

To bait the sites they took dead muskrats and beavers from a 55-gallon drum—that stank to high heaven—and they put those carcasses in a burlap bag and hung them from a tree so the bears could smell the dead animals.

The guide told us the bears generally would not come into the camps, but we should be careful because there were a lot of wolves and they weren't afraid of people. In the daylight, we could tell there were many wolves near our camp because of all the wolf dung. It was so bad we wouldn't even walk in that area. And these were big wolves: We could see their tracks and their dim outlines in the shadows. We could also hear them howling at night so we knew they weren't far away.

Regardless how much experience I had hunting in the Adirondacks and other places, I have to say I just wasn't prepared for the Canadian wilderness. I ended up committing a beginner's error and getting lost for the first time in my life.

The Canadian landscape is totally different than the Adirondacks. In the Adirondacks I could look at the terrain and know whether it is north or south by the steepness of the mountain. One side is a slope and the other side is a cliff, so I can know what is north and south just by the mountains. I don't even have to look for the moss on the north side of the tree to know which direction is north.

Another thing I can do in the Adirondacks is listen for the sound of the sea planes, because I know which lakes the planes take off from and land on. In the fall everybody is up there going for airplane rides to see the leaves. So between visually observing the landscapes and listening for the planes, I pretty much knew where I was at all times.

As I mentioned earlier, I was the guy with the baiting area the furthest out. When it was around noon one day, I decided to go out and set some bait at my site, so I scooped some dead muskrats from the 55-gallon drum, put them in a burlap bag, and took the boat to my assigned area. My plan was to set the bait around 1 p.m. and then come back around 4 and climb a tree and hunt until dark. When I reached my site, however, I saw that a big bear, maybe four or five hundred pounds, had just come through. The tracks were huge and fresh, so I was excited to jump on its trail and hunt it down. It had warmed up to the fifties that day, so I had left my jacket at the campsite. I hadn't figured on being gone for long. Since I had my rifle with me I thought, *Why let it get away?* So I started tracking the bear, hoping to see or hear it moving through the woods. The only problem was that I made a beginner's mistake and forgot to take a compass reading from the place I was leaving. You should always do that so you know the exact spot for the return.

After 45 minutes I realized I had been on this hunt too long without taking any compass readings or getting a view of where I was. I had my backpack with me, so I stopped and I got my compass out; I looked around and nothing looked familiar. In Boy Scouts they teach you to climb a tree to see your surroundings from a higher elevation. This way you can usually see a river or a lake somewhere and figure out where you are. So I climbed a pretty tall tree, and when I looked out the landscape was exactly the same in every direction. All I saw were these mounds with no peaks. What made it even more confusing was that they were all about the same height and there were no outstanding trees. I also did not see any water anywhere. Immediately I realized I had made a big mistake.

By that time it was around 1:45, so I decided to break off the hunt and try to backtrack to the baiting site. Normally, I would leave signs for myself on a hunt like this and break twigs off trees so I could see where I had been, but I hadn't done that. Up here the guide told us that they mark trails by taking a knife and peeling back the bark. If you got lost at night, you would see the spots that were cut because the sap was fluorescent, and you would see them in the moonlight or when you shone your flashlight on the trees.

I didn't see any of those signs, so I took the fluorescent orange ribbons that I had in my backpack and began tying them on the branches of the trees every so many yards. I figured if I really did get lost someone would come and see those ribbons and eventually find me. I did that for an hour and then the unexpected happened —I made a full circle and saw the first ribbons that I had tied. I couldn't believe it. This had never happened to me before. A cold sweat broke out on my forehead and I could feel a rising panic trying to get hold of me. I also understood that the compass I had with me was utterly useless because I had no fixed position to go back to.

It was the same thing with the trail. They say that you always have one leg that is stronger than the other and there is a tendency to walk in circles. Well, that is exactly what happened to me. Now it was 2:45 p.m. and I was convinced—I was lost. Often when panic hits you, there is a sudden impulse to run. You falsely think that you will make up for lost time by running. If you run in the wrong direction, however, the only thing that does is get you twice as lost.

This fear was a new feeling for me in the woods, and it was the first time I was thinking that things might not work out well. My error of not wearing a coat also hit me. This was September, and the temperature dropped to below freezing when it got dark.

I also remembered one night when I was coming home in the dark alone. Usually I would go out with another guy so we only had to take one boat, but on this particular night he had decided to stay at the camp and I went out by myself. After I had spent some time in the woods hunting without seeing anything, it got dark and I started back to the boat. On my way back, however, I heard the rustling of footsteps behind me. I stopped and heard two or three steps, then silence. I tried it again and I could hear the same extra few steps and then quiet. It sounded like only one animal, and I knew it must be an Alpha wolf on the prowl. It felt strange that I, the hunter, was now being stalked as game. I figured if he charged I could get a shot off, so I wasn't that scared, but still it was a bit unsettling to know that to him I was nothing but a large food item. When I got to the little meadow just before the water, I knew he wouldn't come into the clearing. If he did I would have nailed him. He just watched from the shadows as I started the motor. He retreated back to his domain and I went to mine.

So here I was lost in northern Canada with no jacket. It would be dark in a couple of hours. I had just walked around in a circle putting orange ribbons on the trees. Another concern went through my head: What if a bull moose came down the path with an attitude? It is not uncommon for a moose to attack anything that is in its territory. I knew it was a moose trail because it was covered with huge moose tracks. It was also a foot deep because of the weight of the moose traveling on it (they could easily be 1200 pounds), and I assumed it was probably their main route to the water.

Suddenly I was so overwhelmed with all the negative possibilities that I sank down to my knees and told God the obvious: *Lord, I'm lost. Please help me and get me out of here.* Shortly after praying that prayer the panic left me, and I was sure that God heard me because I could feel His peaceful presence.

When I got up I just followed the trail through the woods. After some distance I saw this huge boulder that must have been ten feet high. On top of it I saw an old deteriorated canoe. Someone apparently had put it up there. Who knows why, or when? I figured if I was stuck out there for the night I could use the boulder as a shelter and build a fire to keep the wolves away.

I walked for another half hour and I began thinking that I should have been by the river by now. Normally the ground would start to slope and get flatter as I approached the water but the terrain didn't seem to be changing, so I gave up and turned around and headed back toward the boulder. I now figured the odds were I would be staying there for the night. When I went in the other direction I had gone around the swamp side of the brush, but this time I went into the wooded section instead. As I looked up I saw a white round patch cut out of one of the trees, indicating the trail. I was elated to know I was going in the right direction. After about

15 minutes I started recognizing the scenery, and I knew I was only 20 minutes from the boat. I looked at my watch and it was 4:30. I knew it was too late to go to the camp and get my equipment and return, so I just called it a day. I was physically and mentally exhausted from the ordeal.

The next day the guide came over to our camp, and I told him my story of getting lost and showed him on the map that was laminated into the dining room table where I had been. I was surprised to see that if I had continued on the moose trail I would have eventually come to the water. It was no more than a half mile away. As I was going out with the boat I saw a big opening where that trail would have come out. But, who knows? It could have been more dangerous trying to work my way back to the boat from that spot since the river was a fast moving body of water.

When I spoke with the guide he confessed to me that they had lost people up where I was. He said, "You can go east, west, or south to get found. If you go north we will never find you, because it is too vast and there is nothing out there. By taking the other ways they always ran into another hunter, fisherman, or somebody. But if they went north we never found them."

During the week, Dan was the only one to get a bear. The rest of us still had a phenomenal time fishing and enjoying the Canadian outdoors. It seemed like the fish had never seen a lure or a fly before, and they attacked whatever we threw in the water. We caught all kinds of trout and salmon and Dan was glad to cook them up for us.

There were also leeches in the lakes. I avoided them by taking my bath at daybreak. The other guys made the mistake of dipping in the lake after the sun was up. They would come out of the water with these five-inch leeches on them. And it took some pulling to pluck those bloodsuckers off. I was used to seeing two-inch leeches, but five inches! They were enormous. It took some doing, but we always plucked them off without doing too much damage to the guy's skin. Just looking in the water, we could see scores of them spiraling up to the surface to bath in the warmth of the sunlight.

At the end of the week we made our way back to the train station, loaded up all our gear with the bear, and drove back to the border. Eight hours later, we were informed by the border agent that we couldn't cross the border with the bear because we didn't have the correct permits. It was about four o'clock in the morning and all of us were whipped. There was no way I was going to travel another eight hours back to where we'd been to get a permit. I just told the man, "Okay, fine, sir. Then we'll just leave the bear right here." Of course Dan was horrified that I could be that carefree with his bear, but I was serious. I explained calmly to the customs officer that we had been on a guided hunt and had done everything they had told us to do, and they'd never said anything about needing a permit to get a bear across the border. But if he insisted, I would leave the bear in Canada.

"But you can't do that," he said.

"Oh, yes I can," I replied. "Just watch me."

I think the absurdity of the whole thing struck him at that point. There was no one around. It was early in the morning and he could tell that we weren't purposely trying to break the law. We couldn't go back and he certainly didn't want us to dump a dead bear anywhere.

"All right. Go ahead," he said, as he closed his eyes and just waved us on.

I didn't hesitate. I hit the gas and we were gone.

Searching for the Elusive Ten-point Buck

I have taken so many deer over the years that I've stopped hunting for ordinary deer. What I hunt for now is a trophy deer, which is a buck with at least a 24-inch spread between the front tines and ten or more points. Those deer exist, but to find them is extremely difficult because for a deer to live that long they have to know how to hide themselves. Ninety-five percent of the deer people get hunting are less than three years old.

I have missed two trophy deer in my life. Once was that time with Skip near my camp in the Adirondacks, and the second time was in the Southern Tier, near the southern border of New York, when I was with my brother-in-law Mike and the winds were blowing about 40 mph. We were on a thousand acre tract of land owned by a friend near Binghamton and I was up in a four-foot diameter tree that was swaying in the wind. That's the kind of day it was. Because of the wind, I thought maybe I could get a steadier aim if I was on the ground, so I climbed down. Just as I got to the ground five or six deer strolled into view. Moments later, this magnificent ten-point buck comes out—about 60 yards away. I had this buck sighted and normally I could hit a half a dollar with this gun at 125 yards away. It was a single shot Thompson Contender and it shot a .35 caliber cartridge. It was a powerful gun that I had taken down other nice bucks with before. So I took three shots at this ten-point deer and I missed every time. I just couldn't hold my pistol straight because it was blowing so hard. Every time I extended my arm to shoot, the wind would buffet it.

The buck, of course, didn't even notice I was shooting at him. It was mating season and he apparently was more concerned about which doe in the group was going to be his mate. After my three shots he just sauntered back into the heavy pines. What I should have done after the second round was just grab the 12-gauge shotgun with the scope from Mike and dropped him. Mike didn't shoot because he already had his deer, and he didn't think I would miss with the pistol. By the time Mike and I got to the pines where the buck had disappeared, we could see by the terrain there was no way we could get close enough to them without them seeing us or picking up our scent. We just stood silently as they moved out of range.

Appreciating the Wonder of Creation

Nowadays, going for the trophy deer is a good excuse for me to walk in the woods and observe God's glory, and watch nature do its thing. In West Amboy there are thousands of acres of state land, and I like to hunt up there. In fact, I have taken a number of friends there who got to shoot their first deer. It is just a beautiful section of the woods. I remember walking down there one fall day when the sun was shining and I was totally alone. Suddenly, it was as though I had entered a green paradise. I was dazzled with all the different shades of green. I never realized until that day just how many different tones of green there are. There were the Pine Tree greens and the fern greens and the grass greens. It was amazing. I felt like it was a show just for me. I stood and marveled for a long time at the beauty of it all.

There are some swamps up in the Adirondacks, and I walk through them because I love them. They're called peat bogs and you can walk on top of them, and it's soft and feels like you're walking on a mattress. And there are so many different colors of wild flowers. You would think because it is sometimes a harsh environment a lot of things would not grow, but, on the contrary, the number of different flowers in the Adirondacks blows me away. I go up on those peaks and I can see for forty or fifty miles. Sometimes you even get a day where they say at the airport that there is "unlimited visibility." I flew out to Albany one day for fun, and while I was coming back I could literally see Oneida Lake from Albany. The guy with me didn't believe me when I said, "Do you see that little glimmer on the horizon? That's Oneida Lake."

He said, "Yeah, right. You can't see that far."

I said, "You keep your eye on that little glimmer, and you will see as we get closer to it that it's Oneida Lake." And it was.

The same thing happens up in the Adirondacks. Sometimes you get a day where it seems as if you can see forever—even fifty miles away—and you can see swamps with beautiful designs and colors and mountain ranges that are so far away they look purple. The color and texture of the landscape is just amazing.

I have flown airplanes in the fall just to see the colors from the air. I remember one season I took a few neighbors up to take photos, and the leaves were so colorful that it didn't look real. It looked as if someone had taken a paintbrush and made masterful strokes because they were so bright and vibrant.

Usually you get that only a few days out of the year, because often the sky is overcast or there are clouds or mist or fog, but every now and then you will come across a day that has unlimited visibility and the view is spectacular.

Another memorable experience I've had was when I was flying down the coastline in Florida. At five hundred feet I could see these huge schools of fish called Silver Jacks and see other fish coming in to feed off them. From the air they look like rolling, massive black balls. However, when I saw them from the shore this same school of fish would look like a giant rainbow as they were jumping in and out of the water, fleeing from their predators.

Talking about the beauty of nature, Char and I made a once-in-a-lifetime trip to Alaska, and that is really a final frontier. Maybe I'll talk about that adventure another time. One thing I have noticed is that it is getting harder and harder—even in the Adirondacks—to get to uninhabited places where you can't hear the sounds of cars or trains or trucks or anything civilized. If you have never been to a place by yourself in nature where all you hear are the sounds of the wild, you are missing something extraordinary.

CHAPTER 14
THE RACE IS MORE THAN A TROPHY

For a long time I considered being self-sufficient, independent and being able to do everything myself a good thing. I would go hunting, fishing, and boating by myself. I repaired as many things as I could at home. I had my own business. I had reached the place I thought I wanted to be and, frankly, it was all a delusion. When I thought my marriage was about to collapse nothing else mattered. I didn't want to live without Char, my children, or God in my life. I think being a man is coming to that place in your life where the important things are the basics like your family and doing what you believe is right. It's not the material things or being popular.

It's funny the things by which some people gauge success. Coming from a poor family I always judged my success in material terms, and that's one of the reasons I wanted a nice car and a nice house and a big boat. Once I had them, most of what they brought into my life were more hassles. Boats, I found out, were probably the biggest aggravation because they require so much maintenance. In other words, the fantasy is always better than the reality.

A lot of times we don't really understand what is important to us until we lose it, or think we have. And that can apply to anything—our job, our health, our family, our freedom.

Our relationships with our children we can take for granted too. But what if they weren't there? People lose children every day. I know what that pain is like to some degree, because I thought I had lost my son for three days when he was 22. I truly thought he had died. It was after 9/11, and he had just finished college and had gone to Costa Rica alone. After the attacks on the Twin Towers his flight had been postponed two weeks, and the airline had offered him his money back, but he declined to take it—despite the fact that all his friends did. He was determined to go anyway.

Once he was down there, however, everything did not go as planned. The taxi driver took him to a slum hotel instead of to the one where he had made a reservation. It was also in the middle of the night and the people around him looked dangerous. In fact, he called me and told me about his situation and added: "Dad, there are no locks on my doors."

I agonized that whole night. I felt powerless to help him. I was too far away. I figured, too, for my son to be scared, things had to be serious. He was a big kid who could usually handle himself physically, but how do you guard yourself against someone coming in the middle of the night and slitting your throat? I was devastated.

For two days I waited for news from him, and when I didn't hear anything I concluded that he was dead. Char and I contacted a number of people we knew to pray for him. I also called the Assemblies of God district office and asked if they knew of any missionaries down there who could try to find my son. The director said there was someone, and I gave him the address of the hotel where Jonathon was supposed to be. He said they would call the missionary and see what he could do.

Regardless of all the prayers going up for him, I sank into a depression because I had believed a lie that my son was already dead. Nothing was the same. It was like my world had changed forever. The shows on TV and the songs on the radio were empty. At work I was just going through the motions. There was no joy in anything and nothing could comfort me. It was so devastating to my soul that I felt like I was grieving already for his loss.

Meanwhile, unbeknownst to me, God was answering our prayers. The third morning I received a call from the missionary who said

Jonathon had gone to the hotel, but he had left. I was relieved he had made it out of the other hotel, but still concerned that we had not heard anything from him since that day. That evening Jonathon called and explained everything he had been through. One incident included taking a wrong bus for eight hours into the jungle and back, instead of to a local tourist destination.

Jonathon told me later that he had met up with a man and his family who invited him to come and camp out on their property, which was across the bay. The father was also a soccer enthusiast, so he and Jonathon hit it off immediately. He even took Jonathon with his family to a local soccer game.

When Jonathon came back after ten days it was like the prodigal son returning home. I was so grateful to have him back, I invited him to go on an extended kayaking trip with me—just the two of us. We went to the Adirondacks and did Seventh Lake and Eighth Lake as well as Racket Lake. We found an island and made our camp there. It was great to reconnect with him in such a peaceful environment and one I'd grown to know intimately over the years from my many hunting and fishing expeditions.

The funny thing is, I never tried to force my interests on my kids when they were younger. I felt the outdoor life was my personality and what I liked to do. Of course, I did take them both out with me a couple of times, but once I saw they didn't like something, I didn't force them to do it again. For example, I used to take Jonathon with me to the gun clubs to shoot because I wanted him to be familiar with guns. I felt it was important that he learned under my supervision just how dangerous they were and to respect them. I think, because of that, both of my children were never curious to go sneaking behind my back and get into my gun cabinet.

But during Jonathon's college years, we had definitely lost touch. He, like many others his age, just threw dad's rules and ideas to the wind and sought out for himself what the world had to offer. I understood, because I'd been there, but I had hoped he wouldn't make the same mistakes I had. I was grateful during that time we had together in the Adirondacks that Jonathon felt comfortable enough to unload all the things he was carrying on his conscience and confess some things that he wasn't proud of. Although as a dad I wasn't necessarily thrilled to hear all the details, I knew it was important that he got it off his chest, and that time brought us closer than we had been in years. At one point during our kayaking trip I asked him, "What do you want to do in life?" When he responded that he didn't know I said, "Well, why don't you come and work for me?" He thought for a moment and then said, "Okay. I can give that a shot, I guess."

Now Jonathon is thirty-one, and he is my right hand man here at the shop and in training to take over the business when I retire. He's great with people and I can't think of anyone with whom I'd rather leave it.

CHAPTER 15
DEVELOPING A WINNING STRATEGY

It didn't take long after I started my own business to figure out that God was blessing it. I knew that it was more than just my skills as a manager, because I was aware of many shops out there that had been at it for years and were still struggling with a three-bay shop and a couple of employees. I had gone from a three-bay shop to an eight-bay shop and from two employees to 15 employees in three years. Knowing the law of reciprocity or the principle of sowing and reaping, I understood that in order to prosper I needed to sow. To me, that meant not only giving to the church but also to others in the community as we felt led.

To give you an example, I remember one time feeling compelled to tell our pastor that I thought the Lord had told me that someone from the church needed a brake job done and He wanted me to do it. Although he couldn't think of anyone off hand, shortly afterwards he walked into his secretary's office and heard her talking with someone on the phone, and he noticed that she was upset. When she was done, he asked her what the problem was and she said, "My husband just told me that the brakes went on the car. The timing is really bad because we don't have the money right now to cover that extra expense."

He immediately thought of me and I was thrilled that I had heard clearly from the Lord, and we were happy to help her out.

But it doesn't have to be someone we know in order to help

them. I just try to listen to the leading of the Lord and obey what He tells me. Sometimes I haven't a clue who the people are or what their background is.

I think it helps a lot, too, to have people praying regularly for your business. Once you are in a close-knit church family you form close relationships with people, and it helps tremendously to call on them for prayer support, especially when things are not going well, or when you are facing some challenges. Over the years I've learned in business that things can change on a dime. For example, employees can leave, the economy can plunge, and even the weather can have an effect.

It helps, too, to have people who keep me properly focused and accountable. It's been my experience that it's wise to seek out people who have more knowledge than I have—and that pertains to everything from the automotive field to my spiritual walk. It's easy to get caught up in all the little details of a business, or life for that matter, and forget that seeking His kingdom is the priority, not the business. In all businesses, I think, there are financial ups and downs. Most people go out of business in a year and many more in five years and even a larger percentage in ten years. We have been fortunate to be here still after more than 20 years. Sometimes we've had to persevere in prayer and just keep going in the midst of some pretty tough circumstances, but God has been faithful.

That is not to say that there haven't been some trials along the way and there are some that may be particular to the car repair industry. It's bad enough that the manufacturers change designs and parts almost on a monthly basis, which can create all kinds of mind-boggling situations, but then you also have to deal with the customer service side, which sometimes lands you in court. I have always tried to do the right thing, so when this happens it's hard not to take it personally as an attack on my integrity. I had an extreme case where I was sued for just looking at a customer's car when I hadn't charged him anything and hadn't even done any work on it. These are the kinds of things I found I needed to give to the Lord, or else my heart could turn sour and cynical towards helping people. This is one of the reasons that we try to concentrate on things that we excel at and try not to be all things to all people.

Other trials have been of my own making. One time we were forty grand in the hole and I just didn't know how we got there. All I could do was ask God to help me find out what was wrong, because I had no idea. Char decided to go through the checkbooks with a fine-tooth comb to see what she could find. To me, it didn't seem like we had done anything different and the business was still doing well, so I was bewildered as to how this had happened. This was before the advent of laptop computers and memory sticks, which now make doing these things a lot easier.

As Charlene went through and did a reconciliation of the checkbook, I went through all the invoices of the car parts we were purchasing to see if we were buying more than usual. I told her that I would also take a look at payroll to see if we had missed something or been overcharged by our payroll company. When she was all done she said, "Terry, we have that $40,000 in the checkbook."

I said, "Wait a minute. How is that even possible?"

She said, "It took me a little time to figure it out, but one of our managers made a couple of bank runs at the end of the day and forgot to tell somebody, and the deposits were not entered into the checkbook the next day."

Upon further investigation, I discovered that I had done the same thing as the manager. I was grateful we were okay, but the Lord showed me I needed to know the state of my "flock" or, in other words, to be more diligent about the details of my business. By being forced to re-evaluate the books in some areas, I discovered I did need to cut back on some things: We were a little high in parts, payroll, and with our insurance coverage. The $40,000 shortfall scare, therefore, was a needed wake-up call to better management and I thanked God for it.

In reference to sharing my faith at work, I believe my first responsibility is to give excellent service. If a conversation about my faith comes up I am glad to share what I believe, but I don't feel I need to force people into believing as I do. Sometimes I do get some questions regarding the Hebrew blessing on our doorpost and all the Bibles we have on the counter, but I do not speak of my faith directly unless a customer brings it up, or I feel specifically led by the Lord.

When I renovated the building in 2000, I decided to put a picture on the wall that had a Christian message. I've also done the radio show, The Car Care Clinic for 570 WSYR, for over 16 years, and I share my faith often on the air, so most people know already where I am coming from. For example, at Christmas we give a gospel message at the end of the radio show: At Easter we encourage the men to take their families to church. My co-host, John Metzler, and I talk freely about our lives to make the show more personal and interesting, so our beliefs come out there as well. We don't hesitate to promote worthy church and community events that we feel our listeners might appreciate.

Sometimes we do get some comments about all the Bibles we have in the lobby. Just recently a mother was trying to quiet her teenage daughter, who was mocking the fact that we had Bibles in the office. The mother then turned to us and said, "We are bringing our car here because everyone says how hon…" and she hesitated, as though she was going to say "honest" but changed her mind, and said, ". . . what good technicians you are and what a good job you do."

To create a professional and peaceful atmosphere at my shop, I make sure everybody in my shop understands and implements the following values:

- **Integrity.** Our integrity is everything, and properly diagnosing and repairing the customer's car without selling unneeded parts or repairs is first and foremost.

- **No cursing.** I believe foul language is unacceptable for a professional. It creates a bad environment for other workers and our clients.

- **No drinking on the job.** Nobody comes to work hung over or under the influence of anything. No liquid lunches or imbibing during the workday.

- **No porn or girlie calendars in the shop.** In my opinion, pornography or seductive pictures degrade women, and they are offensive to many people. We prefer car photos.

- **Dress codes and appearance.** You cannot have anything derogatory on your shirts or hats. You must be neat and well groomed and act and look like a professional. Our goal is to be the standard in the industry.

My employees also know where I stand, and I try to bless them whenever I can. To keep good employees I make sure that I pay well for our industry; I also have a bonus system, but it is based on productivity and not on what they sell. This takes the pressure off of being honest or dishonest. When you tell somebody you are going to give a commission check based on what they sell, you get salespeople out there selling people things that they don't need. We also have a bonus based on the profits of the business. We know where our breakeven point is and anything over that the employees get a share. This keeps their focus on quality and productivity and not on sales.

Today's world is different than the one I grew up in. To me work always came first. If I was sick I still showed up. If my car broke down I found a way to get to work and then fixed the car after work. Now there are all kinds of excuses for not showing up and working. In my generation you had to be dead or dying if you didn't come to work. I've seen many young people today who don't even think twice about calling in for all kinds of reasons. Some of them even have their wives call in for them, which I find kind of funny because in my generation you wanted the boss to hear that you were really sick.

My philosophy with boss/employee relationships is to be

friendly and respectful, but not to be their close friend because it can create some sticky situations. Of course, there are always some exceptions to the rule. Generally, I know when there are issues in my employees' lives and I try the best I can to help out. I imagine it is the same with priests and pastors. They have to be friendly to everybody, but they must be careful about not getting too close to too many people, because sometimes they have to correct them. If I am too emotionally invested, I don't think I can be as objective, and it's harder if I do have to challenge them in some area. I feel I have the loyalty of my employees, but that doesn't mean I am an integral part of everything they do. For example, we do celebrate employee birthdays at the office with an ice cream for everybody, but we don't have special parties.

I guess I've said all that to say this: If you want to be at the forefront of your industry, in my opinion, you have to put God first, sow financially into your church and community, find excellent technicians, treat your employees well, focus on what you excel at, and stay abreast of any new developments in your field that can help you be more efficient and productive. One more thing: Don't be afraid to take risks.

CHAPTER 16
SHARING TIPS FOR THE ROAD: GOING ON THE AIR

The Car Care Clinic
AM 570 WSYR
Saturdays 9 to 10 a.m.

I thought a question and answer format might be appropriate for this section of the book about the radio show. The following questions are some that I've been asked throughout the years as well as some I thought you might ask if you were given the opportunity.

How long have you been doing the Car Care Clinic on WSYR and how did it all start?

Believe it or not I have been doing the program for sixteen years. It all started May of 1993. I had a friend, Ed, who worked for WSYR, and one day the program directors were talking about who they were going to get to replace the guys who did this car repair show on Saturday mornings. He just said, "Hey, I know a guy who works on cars. Maybe he'll do it." They gave him a green light and he then called and asked me if I would be interested. When I asked him what I had to do he said: "People will be calling in like they do at your shop. Just answer the questions like you always do."

I said, "I guess I could do that."

When he saw me hesitate he added, "Look. We'll just try it one Saturday and see how it goes."

It sounded like another adventure so I went. In the beginning, I did the show alone. When I got to the station for the first time I was really nervous, and I just about panicked when that red light went on, which meant that I was "live" on the air. My heart started racing and I could hardly breath until I said my first word. Later on, I learned it was necessary to consciously take some deep breaths every now and then or else I would run out of air and not be able to talk at all.

Of course, I also wanted to say the right thing and sound halfway intelligent, but it was a risk not knowing what people were going to ask. What if I didn't know the answer? At first there was just the producer, Ben Bradshaw, and I in the studio. He was working the soundboard, and the plan was if no one called he would ask me some questions. But people kept calling in and I guess I did pretty well because the directors wanted me to continue with the show.

At that time we were doing general repairs as well as transmission work at the shop, so I had exposure to a lot of different scenarios, but as time went by I felt I needed someone more knowledgeable in auto repair. Since I had recently hired John Metzler to be a manager at my shop and he had extensive experience in the automotive field, he seemed the natural choice. He had gone to college for automotive repair, worked at several dealerships, and also had his own business specializing in European cars. After six months on the air, I invited him to join me. He was excited about the opportunity to be on the radio, and his knowledge and personality were a perfect compliment to mine. I thought with my knowledge of transmissions, radiators, and older cars and his expertise in general repairs we would have all the bases covered. At first John was a little intimidated by the show. After his first program he said, "Man Terry, you don't get a lot of time to think about these problems, do you?" I agreed, but it did help to have two people because that gave you more time to think when the other person was talking.

I discovered as well that John would often come up with solutions to the callers' problems that I didn't think of and vice versa.

The listeners benefited, hearing several different possible remedies for the problem instead of only one. I found it was a lot more fun having someone like John there. That way we could keep things hopping. We knew we must have been doing something right, because we always had the highest ratings for our time slot.

Do you have auto repair books with you when you do the program?

No, we don't. We don't have laptops with us either. It's funny, because I see some of the other guys with shows at the station come in with armloads of books. But we just come in and shoot from the hip. But we deal with this stuff every day and between the two of us we have sixty years of experience fixing cars. Now we may not see most of the current year cars with all of their unique problems, but we both do a lot of reading and we get technical service bulletins, so we review those. That way, if someone calls us on the newer cars we can say, "Oh, yeah, we read in one of our trade magazines that this is an issue and this is what you need to do." So, we try to keep up on the industry as much as we can, because there is so much of it out there and things are changing so fast. We also talk back and forth with people at the car dealerships and other repair shops to know what problems they are dealing with. John and I also sit on the Morrisville College Automotive Department Advisory Committee, so we get to hear what goes on at that level. At the school they're dealing with a lot of the new technology and they're teaching all of that, so we get to see what the curriculum is and where the industry is heading.

Maybe you could explain how it works in the studio during the show.

It looks like mission control. You're pretty much inside a glass cage. One side is all glass. There is this huge soundboard in front of you that's all dials and switches where you can adjust your sound and tone. We also have two computer monitors. One has all the upcoming commercials and the other one has the callers' names and questions and what phone line they are on. Of course we have microphones in front of us as well. Then we have these large speakers mounted on the ceiling above us so we can listen to what's going on while we're on break. Normally, we take the calls as they come, but if we get an especially difficult one we may have to put them on hold a little bit so we can discuss it before answering. We can also talk to the producer during the show at any time and he can respond on or off the air. Actually, it is now possible to go on line and watch the show live if you want. Anybody can go to www.terrystransmission.com and to our direct link or go to www.wsyr.com.

Have you ever given some advice on the air that you realized later might be wrong and then felt you needed to correct it on your next show?

No, not really, because we wouldn't know if we were wrong unless somebody told us. We just speak out of our experience in the industry and the answers we give have been solutions in certain cases. A lot of times we have people calling us to let us know that we were right. Often we give callers a number of possible causes for their problem, not a definitive answer, because we can't possibly know that without looking at the vehicle in question. For example, let's say somebody calls and tells me they have a vibration problem. Well, there might be 20 things that could cause that vibration, but I might only be able to think of 12 at the time. We usually start with the most common reasons for the particular problem and then go down the list from there. We're always happy to hear when we get it right, but a lot of the times we don't know if we hit the nail on the head or not. Sometimes other callers will contact us on the show and say that they had the exact same problem with the same model car and what the solution was.

Can you think of any humorous calls that you've received on the show?

We have many callers who have told me that they thought a particular call was very funny. I cannot think of any specific call, but John and I always get a kick out of it when callers make the noises that their cars make. Sometimes we might ask them to say it again if it is particularly amusing. But one thing we don't do is make fun of our callers or talk to them in a condescending way. I've listened to other radio shows where the hosts like to bust on the people who call. They may get a laugh but it is at the caller's expense. We want to do the opposite and communicate to our audience that we really appreciate them for taking the time to call us. The last thing we want to do is to embarrass somebody on the air.

Speaking of similar talk shows that are out there, how would you compare what you do to what they do?

We have always tried to keep our answers simple and to the point—not trying to confuse them with overly technical terms or using jargon the callers wouldn't understand. I have listened to other shows, and I think they joke around too much and the laughing would eventually get on my nerves. But they do have good information. I just enjoy doing our show and I try not to compare it with other people's programs. We have our own style and it seems, according to the ratings, that there are a lot of people out there who like it. Some of our listeners tell us they like us better because we take every question seriously and try to give the best response possible.

Speaking of celebrities, have you had the opportunity to meet many famous people over the years at the radio station?

Probably more than I know. Of course I've met the local famous people like Joe Galuski and Jim Reith. Many times Joe will have special guests for the pre-game sports shows who I will bump into on my way out of the station. Probably the most well known person I've met has been Glenn Beck. I first became aware of him when I was down in Florida and heard his program on the radio. I found him very humorous and a great storyteller. He also didn't seem to be partisan—he busted on the political right as well as the left. When he came to Syracuse for his first Christmas show, I was one of his sponsors and I've been honored to do that each time he's come back. Being a sponsor also gives me an opportunity to spend some time with him before the show begins. Clear Channel always puts on a buffet for Glenn and his sponsors so we have a photo op and time to talk.

My most memorable experience with Glenn was when he came to Syracuse for his book signing tour for *The Christmas Sweater*. He was supposed to hit six cities in one day. At Syracuse his itinerary included the Barnes and Noble bookstore on Erie Boulevard at 10 a.m. The store was going to open up a half hour early, so Char and my son Jonathon decided to go there even earlier. I was planning on joining them after my radio show. However, when the radio show was over and I called them, they discouraged me from coming over because it was raining so hard and there were so many people there. They also said Glenn had not arrived yet. I decided to head home instead, but on the way I thought I would check out the local airport to see if his flight was canceled because the weather was so poor. As a pilot I was familiar with the private side of the airport, so I pulled into the parking lot. I saw a charter bus waiting and figured it was his. I got out of my car and started walking towards the entrance of the Fixed Based Operations. Glenn and his entourage just happened to be walking out at the same time, so I just said, "Hey, Glenn. Looks like you're running a little late." He had his head down because it was raining and he quickly looked up and was surprised to see me. He said, "Oh Terry. Yeah, I am running a little late. Hey, you wanna ride with us?" He took me off guard and I had to think about it for a second, but finally replied, "Yeah. Sure." So we got on the bus and got under way. On the way I called my wife and asked her if she was still in line. She said, "Oh yeah. We're still waiting." I said, "Keep the faith. Glenn and I will be there in ten minutes." She said, "You must be kidding."

"No. I'm on the bus with Glenn and we will be there soon."

This gave me a chance to chitchat with Glenn one on one, as there was no one else vying for his attention. We talked about things in Syracuse and the economy and how things were going for both of us. I have to tell you quite honestly, as famous as Glenn is, he has to be one of the most down-to-earth people I have ever met. He asked me things about Syracuse that you'd have to follow closely to know about, such as the mall project and Lockheed Martin.

As the bus approached Barnes and Noble, Glenn's bodyguard closed all the shades, and when the bus came to a stop he announced that he would get out first and scan the crowd. When he climbed the bus stairs again he told us what order he wanted us to go out in. I was surprised when he said, "Terry, you go first." I just figured the star would be the first one out. Then I started thinking, *Maybe I'm the human shield.* I just descended the steps and looked around and saw the immense crowd with cameras poised but no flashes going off. Someone then said loudly, "That's Terry." Of course that didn't help because they were probably thinking, "Who's Terry?" Later I found out the voice belonged to one of the guys who delivered my parts at the shop.

I made my way into the bookstore and found my family and explained to them what had happened. I was happy that when Glenn signed our book he gave Char a hug and invited us all to stick around after the signing for some personal time. However, after he signed over eight hundred books the police, who were also there, escorted him quickly to the bus. We thought that he had forgotten his invitation, but as we walked up to the bus the door opened and the bus driver said, "You're coming back with us, right?"

I said, "Yes," and Char and I got in and Jonathon drove the car back home. This time I let Char do all the talking, and she asked him more personal things, like how his family was doing and how he was holding up under such a hectic schedule. His security guard kept calling off ETA's to the airport, so we thought it would be good to get a picture of us with him on the bus so we wouldn't waste his time at the airport. When we were almost there I asked him if I could pray for him and he said, "I would like that." I just put my hand on his shoulder and prayed for him and his family's safety, and that he would use his talents for the glory of God. Needless to say, Char and I were on cloud nine the whole day.

Do you find that your listeners are mostly car enthusiasts or can they be anybody?

No. Actually, it can be anybody. Believe it or not, half of our listeners are women. I have a lot of women who come into the shop or call the shop and say, "I listen to you all the time." I also have some men tell me: "My wife makes me listen to you every week." I'm not sure why our program attracts women. It could be because we try to give people a glimpse into our personal lives. For example, we sometimes talk about our families and our wives and what's happening in our churches. On the other hand, we also get calls from professionals when they are experiencing a problem and just want our opinion. Our callers can be from any walk of life.

Have you changed anything with the show since you started sixteen years ago?

The biggest change was bringing John on board, of course, and he has added greatly to the show with his personality and his vast knowledge about cars. For a while John and I shared doing the soundboard, but now he does that exclusively. Somewhere down the road he just took that over. He likes that aspect of it, so I just let him do it. So I just sit back and chime in now and then. John is a good talker and he knows how to keep the conversation lively. He's also good at filling in with small talk when we only have a few minutes or seconds left before a break. This is very important, because when they have an outside feed coming in, like Fox News, the timing has to be perfect.

I have also participated on the show from other locations. It was funny that a listener picked up on that one time. I think he may have heard the sea gulls and the ocean in the background when I was down in Florida for a vacation.

Another time was interesting when I called from a hotel while I was attending a conference and a maid walked in while I was "live" on the show. I couldn't answer her because I was talking on the radio, so she just assumed no one was there and came in. When she saw me she made an immediate retreat and backed out the door.

Another thing that has changed is that *Terry's Transmission* now owns the show. In the beginning I was paid to do the show by WSYR. After a few years they offered me the option to buy it. They also gave me the advertising minutes during the program, so I can sell that time to sponsors to cover the costs of the show. Now you hear that the show is brought to you by *Terry's Transmission*. We are careful about who we let advertise. They have to have a good reputation and have been in the business for a number of years. It's fun to invite our sponsors on the show throughout the year and let people get to know them.

How many listeners do you estimate that you get for the show and how large a radius does it reach?

I think they estimate our radius at roughly 100 miles. It seems to go further north and east. In terms of listeners we estimate it at around 40,000 at any given time.

So, Terry, do you think the Car Care Clinic is going to make it to its 20th anniversary?

The surprising thing about radio is that things can change overnight. You may be on the air this week and off the next. When I started the program 16 years ago, talk radio was a new thing. Now it is the rage and there is a talk show for almost everything you can imagine. The radio station management can also change and the new directors can have a different idea of what programs they want on their station. We have survived three management changes over the last 16 years. I am totally amazed that we have been on the air this long. In fact, I think we have been on 570

WSYR as long as Rush Limbaugh and much longer than Glenn Beck. Of course, they have a different kind of show and make millions doing it, but it's just to say we've paid our dues. I guess as long as we keep enjoying the show and the ratings stay high, we'll be welcome to stay.

In other words, right now you don't have any plans to stop?

Every few years we have to renew our contract with the station and negotiate the deal. Up to now, it has not been difficult to agree on the terms of our contract, but that could change. I'm not looking to retire any time soon. A lot depends on John and what he wants to do because, quite frankly, I rely heavily on John's knowledge. As I've gotten older, I've stepped out of the hands-on stuff, and I'm not so much involved with the repair end of it as I used to be, so it's harder for me to answer some of these questions. I like it when people call with questions about the older cars because I know most of those answers. If John ever decided to leave the show I don't know if we could continue, because he is the guy who knows about the newer cars coming out since he is still dealing with them and I'm not. I'm starting to be more old school, and I just don't immerse myself in that end of it anymore. I'm more involved now in the business end of it as opposed to the repair side. That doesn't mean I don't have some hands-on experience. I still do 90% of the initial test drives of the cars coming into our shop, and I like to drive them after the repairs just to make sure I am satisfied with how they feel. I am just less involved in the actual repair work. If there is a new problem that I have never dealt with before, I am still curious about solving the problem and I will go out and see what I can do. I still like a challenge. Somewhere down the road, though, I might have to get somebody else to take my place who has more knowledge than me. Who knows? Maybe my son will step up to the plate.

EPILOGUE

One thing that is inevitable when you reach the sixth decade of life is the passing of some of your family, friends, and relatives. It's not an easy time, especially when you lose someone close to you. When my dad died in 1997, that was a difficult time. We were not very close when I was growing up because of his hectic work schedule, and we only really connected on a more personal basis during the last years of his life. Unfortunately, he just got caught up in life and work and before he knew it, his kids were out of the house. I really appreciated those last years when he would go out of his way to sit down and talk with me.

One fond memory I have of my dad was when I took him for an airplane ride. My mom and he had come up to see us from Florida, and Rudy and I conspired together to get dad in a plane with me. We both knew he was deathly afraid of small airplanes and would not go willingly, so we invited him to go on an errand with us to the hardware store. We eventually took him to the airport, telling him it was only to show him the plane I flew.

Rudy hopped in the back seat and I jumped in the front seat, and we coaxed him to come in and take a look at all the gauges, switches and instruments. He wasn't too keen on the idea, but he finally got in the plane. As soon as he sat down Rudy reached over his shoulder and shut the door and I fired the plane up and taxied down the ramp. I quickly called the control tower and they cleared me to take off since it was a slow day.

"No. Don't do this!" he said and then just grasped his knees tightly and held on for dear life.

It took dad half an hour to lighten up and enjoy the flight. Finally he started looking around at the instruments and over Oneida Lake where we were flying. The day was perfect for dad with no wind and no clouds in the sky. After an hour I made a smooth landing. Both Rudy and I had to laugh when he told mom how we had kidnapped him and taken him for a plane ride. Instead of feeling sorry for him she just said, "I wish I had gone."

After he retired and moved to Florida, I used to go down and visit and we would sit down and chit chat. He let me share my faith with him, and one time I brought over a video of a drama that was presented at Believer's Chapel called, *Heaven's Gates and Hell's Flames*. We watched it together and then discussed it afterwards. It was then that he prayed to ask Jesus into his heart.

Later, when I flew down there to see him before he died, I was encouraged to hear that he would often ask the hospice workers to read to him from the Psalms. It confirmed to me that something deeply spiritual had indeed happened when he prayed with me earlier. It encouraged me as well to know that he sought strength from the word of God during his last days. It was tough for me, though, to sit there day after day and watch him die. Finally, I decided to come home. Two days after my arrival in Syracuse, he died.

After his death, however, I was troubled by a lot of things. He was only 71, and I was disappointed that I didn't get to spend more time talking with him about his life and all the things he had learned. He was a talented man in many ways, and I would have liked to ask him more questions about all the things he knew. For example, I had seen him convert buildings into businesses, apartments, and residences. He could walk into a building and tell you the best way to remodel it off the top of his head without putting anything to paper. Unfortunately, the lines of communication between us weren't that open when I was younger. Maybe because of that lack in my life, I have always made it a point to talk to my kids about different things. We've had all kinds of little talks. When they were small we'd have talks about how to behave in public places. When they were older I talked with them about peer pressure and the temptations to drink and the possible consequences of premarital sex. I wanted to let them know directly from me about some of the pitfalls in life and how to avoid them.

Yet, with my own dad, I didn't experience that so I felt cheated in a way. I guess you could say that I was grieving over the fact that our time together on earth had elapsed before we really got to know each other as adults.

But then I had a dream that changed everything. In the dream my dad and I were in our family trailer, sitting on the couch in the living room. It seemed like we had talked for hours and hours. I don't remember the details of our conversation, but I felt an incredible peace. When I woke up the peace was still there and that sense of sadness and grieving was lifted. I just knew that my dad was with God and that I was going to see him again.

Before ending this book, I'd like to share a true experience that took place while I was leading the men's ministry at Brewerton Assembly of God Church. I have chosen this story to end with because I think it reveals something about God's character that many people fail to see for some reason—His passionate desire to be intimate with us and involved in the details of our lives.

It was winter and I had scheduled a snowmobiling trip for the men's group. I loved the outdoors and I knew a number of men who would not dare go to church but who would love to go snowmobiling. So I had a small group of six guys, both Christian and non-Christian, and we were all gathered in front of the church. They had their snowmobiles on trailers and they were ready to go. We had a big problem though—there was not very much snow. Most of the snow had melted because of unusually warm weather, and although it was snowing that day, there was little snow on the ground.

I was convinced in my heart that we would have enough snow, so I just told everyone that we would drive up to Sandy Creek because there was always snow there. In our group, however, there was a guy with a brother who lived in Sandy Creek, so he said, "I've got a brother who lives up there. I've got my cell phone, so I'll just call and ask him before we go if there is snow up there."

He dialed the number of his brother and after a few minutes said, "He says it's snowing up there but there isn't much on the ground. We probably have more than they do right here in Central Square."

This didn't damper my spirits at all and I said, " Well, I think the Lord will provide. Let's go anyway."

Everybody sided with me except this one guy. He just said, "I'm not going to waste my time. I just called my brother and he said there wasn't enough snow." So he left, probably believing we were all out of our minds. The rest of us just started on our way and lo and behold, while we were traveling up there, it started to snow so hard we could hardly see where we were driving. By the time we got up to Sandy Creek the ground was covered with plenty of snow.

As we pulled into the parking lot we also saw three other guys there in their cars with snowmobiles on their trailers. One of the guys rolled down his window and said, "Hey, we're all from Binghamton and we want to go snowmobiling, but we don't know the area and it's snowing so hard we're afraid we may get lost. Do you mind if we go with you guys?"

I said, "Sure, no problem. I know the area."

So we all fired up our snowmobiles and took off down the trail. The only problem was, I was the lead snowmobile and after half a mile it was snowing so hard I could hardly see. I also realized that if I could hardly see they were seeing even less since the sleds were kicking up snow. I stopped my snowmobile and explained to them the problem: "Guys, I'm afraid someone is going to have an accident and may get hurt if we keep going like this." And for the benefit of the guys from Binghamton I said, "We are a Christian men's group and we believe in the power of God, so I am just going to pray that God stops the snow so we can see clearly."

My group bowed their heads with me and I asked God: "Lord, thank you for your answer to prayer to give us snow. I ask you now to stop it from snowing so hard so nobody gets hurt and we can see and have a good time together. Amen."

Immediately, we got back on the sleds, fired them up, and it wasn't 60 seconds later that the sun came out and it stopped snowing. We continued on and made this big loop that took about an hour and then came back and ate lunch. We had enough for everybody, so we invited the guys from Binghamton to join us. After lunch we went out for another couple of hours. It was beautiful and the snow conditions were perfect, so we made the most of the time and we followed many trails in different areas. No one had an accident and no one got hurt. We just zipped along enjoying ourselves without a care in the world. As we loaded up the snowmobiles to go home, the guys from Binghamton thanked us profusely.

As soon as we got loaded up, however, the snow started to fall in thick, heavy flakes. In fact, it snowed so hard that our trip, which normally took 35 minutes, took us an hour and a half because we had almost zero visibility.

I don't know how that whole experience affected those guys from Binghamton, but there was one non-Christian guy with us, whose wife went to our church, who couldn't get over how God stopped the snow for us. He was just amazed how God could care about everything we do—even a snowmobile ride. To him it was almost like the Red Sea parting—he was that impressed. He couldn't believe how quickly the snow stopped and stayed stopped for the whole time we were snowmobiling. He said he just didn't realize how much God cared. Later, he gave his life to Christ as a result of that experience. It blesses me to no end that God even used that adverse weather to bring someone to Himself. It goes to show that God can use anything.

What is interesting is that I had tried to witness to this guy before but nothing ever seemed to move him. One time we invited him and his wife to come over to our camp in the Adirondacks to watch a video about a famous drag car racer named Big Daddy who came to the Lord. I thought because he liked racing this might touch him, but he just seemed uncomfortable and nervous at the end, as if we were going to jump on him. Instead, God used a demonstration of His power so this man would see how much He loves him.

Maybe you've reached this point in the book and all the God talk just doesn't add up for you. Perhaps you've gone through some rough times yourself, or someone has hurt you so bad that you cannot forgive him or her. Maybe your marriage is on the rocks like mine was. Maybe you have a wayward son or daughter and you wonder if they will ever straighten out. Maybe you have a loved one who is suffering from a serious illness. Maybe you just cannot forgive yourself for something you have done. If I give only one message in this book it is this: There is hope for every circumstance because God exists, and He cares about you and your situation. He's helped me on numerous occasions and He is not a respecter of persons.

If any of those scenarios apply to you, it might be helpful to go back to that time that I was lost in the woods up in Canada. I saw myself as a self-sufficient and competent outdoorsman, but I had made some very elementary mistakes like not bringing a coat with me and not taking a compass reading. I also panicked. It was only when I got down on my knees and admitted to myself that I was lost that I found peace. So it is when we begin a relationship with God. We can't find a Savior if we don't believe we are lost. The beginning of a wonderful relationship with our Creator starts here. Simply admit to God you are lost. Invite Him into your heart and life by faith. Get into His word and talk with Him and listen to His voice. Find a Bible-believing church and get involved.

Wherever you are in your life, from zero to sixty or beyond, don't let all that God has planned for you pass you by.

"Do you not know that in a race all the runners run,
but only one gets the prize? Run in such a way as to get the prize."
(1 Corinthians 9:24)

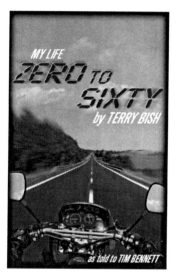

To order more copies of
My Life: Zero to Sixty,
please visit
www.terrystransmission.com

Breinigsville, PA USA
14 December 2009
229172BV00002B/2/P